HIDDEN IN PLAIN SIGHT

A Visitor's Guide to the Hidden Symbolism of Sacramento's
Public Buildings

Gary R. Varner

An OakChylde Book/Lulu Press Publication

ISBN: 978-1-105-35560-8

An Oakchylde Book
Published in the United States by Lulu Press, Inc.

CONTENTS

Introduction   4

A Note on Architectural Styles   7

Grotesques, Greenmen and Monsters   8

What Are Grotesques & Green Men?   10

Mermaids   34

A Bestiary   46

Afterword   72

Appendix: Figure Locations   73

Bibliography   75

Index   84

INTRODUCTION

Ancient symbolism continuously influences the lives of everyone, in every society, throughout time. This is because symbols are important to each generation and seem to be imbedded in the psyche. Symbols satisfy a need to be linked to an ancient tradition and the physical remains of that tradition. Overtime these symbols, and the various things they represent, become absorbed into the dominating culture and religion and come to represent the core values of those cultures and religions. This is especially obvious in the development of Christianity.

"Classical mythology," wrote E.P. Evans "was another source from which Christian symbolism derived many conceptions and forms subsequently embodied in ecclesiastical architecture. [Gentile converts] ...were also told that the pagan religions were not merely old wives' fables, but had a certain heavenly origin and historical justification as preparatory to Christianity, which they foreshadowed." [1]

Symbologist J.C. Cooper noted that "Symbolism is not only international, it also stretches over the ages; it has 'the virtue of containing within a few conventional lines the thought of the ages and the dreams of the race. It kindles our imagination and leads us to realms of wordless thought.' (Lin Yu-tang)." [2]

The symbols and strange images we have today that are found in our cemeteries, on our religious structures, our banks and in our parks are the same symbols that have been part of the framework of the human psyche for thousands of years. While contemporary man of the 21st century may think that they are simply decorative

---

[1] Evans, E.P. *Animal Symbolism in Ecclesiastical Architecture.* London: W. Heinemann 1896, 18.
[2] Cooper, J.C. *An Illustrated Encyclopaedia of Traditional Symbols.* New York: Thames and Hudson 1978, 7.

manifestations of a by-gone era, they represent so much more. They represent the fears, dreams, ideas, beliefs and struggles that humankind has endured since we began to walk upright. This book will survey many of the icons that still reside alongside modern man and will give a meaning for them both in the context of ancient history and folklore as well as a meaning that is suitable for our contemporary times.

Dragons, gargoyles, mythical beasts and strange carvings of foliate faces are all around us. Ancient symbolism is as much a part of our lives as the newest Chryslers, Fords and Jaguars. Symbolic images of ancient design and meaning can be found not only on ecclesiastical buildings of the Old World, but also on Victorian and contemporary buildings in the New World. While in America many of these motifs are seen in historic structures dating from the mid 1800's to the early 1900's, the periodic revival of "pagan" feelings in the last few years, as they did during the Gothic Revival in Victorian England, has created a newfound awareness of these archetypes. Gargoyles, "Green Men," and other representations of ancient elemental spirits and ancient symbols can be found in most of the older American cities. They can also be found in newer neighborhoods, if they are not part of the architecture their likenesses can be purchased in garden shops, craft stores and museum shops.

The recent resurgence of these images appears to reflect the fluid nature of the human psyche that occurs in society. The sacredness of the earth, the universal attachment to ancient myth, the knowledge that "something" is missing in our lives, and that so much of our natural world is in danger of extinction has re-established an attachment to our past. A past that is re-surfacing through an awareness of our linkage to religions and traditions that once dominated the world and greatly influenced who we are.

We have a psychic connection with these representatives of the ancient archetypes, even though so many of them may also, to some, represent our darkest nightmares. The primitive visages that we see looking down upon us from an old building somehow bring a certain level of comfort as well as awe to us. That is unless one has been programmed to see evil in anything unusual or otherworldly. Many people will be surprised that so many examples of these ancient symbols can be found near where they tread, on the façades of apartment buildings, government agencies and churches in the middle of Sacramento. However, if one were to look up more often, he or she may be amazed at the wondrous sights that have been patiently awaiting them.

Why or how these images came to be part of California's architecture is subject for discussion. Perhaps they were a decorative fad at one time or functioned as metaphors for a troubled time. Regardless of their origins, they existed in the dawn of time and remain in man's universal unconsciousness—occasionally rising over time through the works of artisans and masons. This book will provide pictorial examples of the images as well as any available historical information. In addition, we will attempt to provide the reader with the original meaning of the images as found in folklore, presented in a historical and religious perspective.

Our overall focus is to provide a record of these images before they are destroyed in "redevelopment" efforts, or simply crumble into dust. It is hoped that Green Men and grotesque aficionados will find the photos and information contained in this volume of interest and of use in their own studies. A list of the street addresses where the images photographed in this book and others can be found is located at the end of the book.

Gary R. Varner
Sacramento

A NOTE ON ARCHITECTURAL STYLES

The stone carvings depicted in this book are representative of several architectural styles dating back to the mid-nineteenth century in America. Several "revival" styles such as the Greek and Gothic Revival style and the Italianate style were born out of Victorian England as a result of the Industrial Revolution and the desire of people to recapture the "Golden Age" in styles evocative of a past greatly embellished and romanticized.

The Gothic Revival style was heavily inspired by medieval forms and the Green Men and grotesques discussed in this book are a direct result of that architectural mindset.

Like many other American cities populated in the mid 1800's Sacramento became the home of immigrants from around the world. Explorers, gold seekers, sailors, artisans and businessmen from China to Great Britain settled in this area and not only brought their languages and strength but also their art, skills and beliefs. All of these things resulted in the architectural marvels we have today that still exist along the East Coast, the Mid West and West Coast in metropolises such as Des Moines, San Diego, San Francisco and Sacramento.

The majority of the images discussed in this book, which can still be seen and experienced in Sacramento were created between 1850 and 1930 in the heyday of the Gothic Revival period that grew out of the Victorian age. This was a time of exploration, exploration not only of continents and seas, but of ideas and expression. It was also a time when the past was thought to be the Golden Age and ancient and mystical artistic expressions were embraced in an attempt to transport the rapidly industrialized nation into a more sensitive, expressive and mythical one with roots deeply set into the mysteries of nature.

GROTESQUES, GREEN MEN & MONSTERS

Grotestques, Green Men and other strange, monstrous beasts which reside in and on some of Europe's most famous churches and cathedrals also seem to have taken up residence not only on our own American continent, but in our imaginations and hearts. Over the years they have appeared in movies (*Gargoyles,* the 1972 production starring Cornel Wilde as an anthropologist investigating tales of winged demons in Arizona) and cartoon series as a half-human, ancient race of pseudo-super heroes. Green Men are commonly believed to be gargoyles but, while they share many of the physical locations, they are an entirely distinct species of art and can be regarded as *grotesques* rather than gargoyle. The Green Man's origins, meanings, and even some of his physical qualities have merged with the gargoyles although their paths have long been separate.

Gargoyles and grotesques can take a variety of forms. Dragons, devils, demons, half-human and half-animal are the most common but there are a large number as well that are caricatures of real people or classes of people. The styles and possible meaning and functions will be discussed here. While there is growing interest in these carvings, which originated during the time of ancient Egypt, there is not a large amount of meaningful written material concerning them. In fact, even though the Victorian age was responsible for a huge number of gargoyles during the Gothic Revival period the architects and scholars who were responsible for the revival did not seem to care about the gargoyle's interpretation. There has not been much of an improvement in the 20th and 21st centuries either. Very little has been produced on the history or symbolism of these works of art. Books about Gothic and Romanesque church architecture especially that of France's Notre-Dame Cathedral, have the greatest amount of detail concerning gargoyle and grotesque carvings but as historic accounts they are superficial at best. As Bill Yenne wrote, "there is no accepted explanation of why they exist as they do." [3] The Gothic Revival period produced the largest and most varied number of gargoyles and grotesques—as well as the most beautifully carved—however, the origin of the gargoyle dates much earlier. According to Bridaham, "A gargoyle dug up at Alesia dating from 160 AD, shows a plain channel with a human head as spout." [4]

No two gargoyles are identical even though there were thousands at one time peering down from their lofty heights across Old Europe and Britain and many still exist today, although many of these are reconstructions.

It is unfortunate today that the art of stone carvings has almost died out in the Western World. There is hope however. One school of stone carving still operates in the United States and the master carvers who graduate from there are restoring and creating these magnificent works once again. The modern world would not be the same without these weird, humorous and monstrous objects, which reflect the hidden fears of our soul as well as our ancient past.

[3] Yenne, Bill. *Gothic Gargoyles*. New York: Barnes & Noble Books 2000, 18.
[4] Bridaham, Lester Burbank. *Gargoyles, Chimeres, and The Grotesque in French Gothic Sculpture*. New York: Architectural Book Publishing Co., Inc. 1930, xiv.

WHAT ARE GROTESQUES
& GREEN MEN?

Grotesques are a close, almost identical, cousin of the gargoyle. The main difference is that the grotesques do not act as water spouts—they simply *are*—residing as peculiar and imaginative objects of art upon some of our most interesting architecture. The functional gargoyle does not exist in the architecture of Sacramento but many grotesques do. To get a better understanding of the origin of the grotesque we will look at the history of the gargoyle as well.

The origin and purpose of grotesques has piqued the interests of people ever since they began to appear as architectural motifs. "Where may one find an explanation," asked a nineteenth century reader of the British journal, *Notes and Queries,* "of grotesque figures often seen in old churches, both in *carved* stone and painted glass...And why represented in a sacred edifice?"[5]

St. Bernard of Clairvaux asked the same question in the year 1125:

"Of what use to the brothers reading piously in the cloisters are these ridiculous monstrosities, these prodigies of deformed beauty, these beautiful deformities?... Almighty God! If we are not ashamed of these unclean things, we should at least regret what we have spent on them." [6]

Who Carved These Creatures and Why?

There are a variety of opinions and theories as to how gargoyles and grotesques wound up on ecclesiastical structures such as the magnificent Notre-Dame Cathedral. Many researchers have concluded that the church had them carved to either attract pagans into the fold or, as Evans told us earlier, to warn those heathens what awaited them after death. Others have theorized that the carvers themselves, predominately pagan in their traditions and beliefs,

---

[5] *Notes and Queries*, Vol. 8, 2nd Series, August 13, 1859, pg. 130.
[6] As quoted in *Oxford's Gargoyles and Grotesques* by John Blackwood. Oxford: Charon Press 1986, 2.

freely designed and carved them to make fun of their Christian employers or to endow these Christian buildings with an older, pagan symbolism.

Unfortunately, we may never get a clear and concise history of the carvers, their art or their subject matter. As Piccinini noted, gargoyles have "generally been overlooked in art history studies" and only "occasionally cited in research on single folkloric themes."[7]

Because the gargoyle has been in a continuous state of restoration, (the original gargoyles on Notre-Dame reportedly were destroyed during the French Revolution and completely restored later, beginning in 1830) it is impossible in many instances to determine the original images from the newer ones, much less date them. This also causes some major difficulties for folklorists in attempting to study any thematic connection between gargoyles as well as gargoyles and the structures they inhabit. Although gargoyles most certainly are based on ancient traditions and folklore any attempt to classify themes "and their significance and origins," writes Piccinini, "seems a particularly difficult undertaking, at least for the moment." [8]

Most gargoyles made during the Middle Ages were constructed of limestone, Brabantine sandstone or marble although gargoyles made entirely of lead were common from the 16th century and the Chrysler Building in New York City sports a rookery of art deco stainless steel gargoyles. An example of an early lead gargoyle were those made for the Reims Cathedral in France which were installed after a fire in 1481.

Gargoyles appear to have an evolution all of their own. At first crudely done during the early 12th century, they eventually became more complex with human figures replacing the usual animal fare.

Early writers, as well as many contemporary researchers, believed that gargoyles were a cultural icon left from the ancient pagan past. In an article appearing in the *Gentleman's Magazine* in 1889 the author wrote "I fancy that many of these old carvings on

---

[7] Piccinini, Chiara. "Gargoyles" in *Medieval Folklore: A Guide to Myths, Legends, Tales, Beliefs, and Customs*. Oxford: Oxford University Press 2002, 169
[8] Ibid., 170

gargoyles and fonts are merely traces of a heathenism which lasted on into Christian days—a heathenism which Christianity overlapped and absorbed." [9]

Even Theodore Roosevelt had an opinion about why gargoyles were created. He wrote in 1913, "The makers of the gargoyles knew very well that the gargoyles did not represent what was most important in the Gothic cathedrals. They stood for just a little point of grotesque reaction against, and relief from, the tremendous elemental vastness and grandeur of the Houses of God. They were imps, sinister and comic, grim and yet futile, and they fitted admirably into the framework of the theology that found its expression in the towering and wonderful piles which they ornamented." [10]

Benton agrees with Roosevelt in his assessment. Gargoyles were created, she says, as "yet another form of visual pleasure in medieval life—that of amusement..." She goes on to equate the gargoyle as 'examples of what may appropriately be termed 'medieval mischief,' and go some way to showing us how the inhabitants of the Middle Ages came to terms with and enjoyed their world." [11] As one scholar noted, "Grotesque art, then, expresses the repressed."[12]

However, Benton notes as well that "only occasionally do they represent obvious religious subjects" although they may have been created to act as protectors of the church structure from outside evil or to enforce the belief that hell is not a nice place and certain punishment existed for all sinners. [13]

We are yet faced again with the uncertainty of the very reason *why* the gargoyle was created and the true purpose it served, the

[9] Addy, S.O. "A Yorkshire Village", in *The Gentleman's Magazine*, Vol. CCLXVII, July to December. London: Chatto & Windus, Piccadilly 1889, 34.
[10] Roosevelt, Theodore. *History as Literature and Other Essays.* New York; Charles Scribner's Sons 1913, 308.
[11] Benton, Janetta Rebold. *Art of the Middle Ages.* London: Thames & Hudson Ltd., 2002, 19.
[12] Bienville, Michael de. *Gargoyles.* Kansas City: Andrews and McMeel 1996, 20.
[13] Ibid., 198.

debate over the origin and purpose, if there was one, of gargoyles is likely to be a prolonged one.

How and why many of the gargoyles and grotesques were created at approximately the same time in so similar a fashion, even though hundreds of miles separated the buildings upon which they resided, is one of cultural context. The gargoyles originally appeared in an area approximating the original Celtic world. It may be safe to assume that where the pagan traditions of the Celts existed, so did the gargoyles. It was an unforeseen boon for the stone carvers that the Church was willing to employ them on an extended basis for the construction of the great Gothic cathedrals. What better canvas for the carvers to work with but huge unadorned buildings? Most of the gargoyles and grotesques were fashioned on the ground and hauled into place with the use of a windlass and pulley. While some were carved *in situ,* they usually were the results of planning and careful artistry—models in clay being crafted to ensure that the proper effect was obtained.

To assume that these carvings were created, and then installed, on ecclesiastical buildings without the knowledge and consent of Church leaders would be incorrect. As noted previously, St. Bernard was well aware of them and was highly critical, if not shocked. While this view was common among Orthodox Christians, who declared that such creativity and supporters of the arts were "heathens and pagans",[14] his attitude could not have been universal among the Catholic clergy because, if it were, more than likely the gargoyle makers would have been stopped before their sculptures began to appear in thousands of locations around Europe. As Benton theorized, "Like medieval grotesque art in general, gargoyles may be survivals of pagan beliefs the Church permitted to persist besides Christian subjects, incorporated into church decoration for superstitious reasons." [15]

Hundreds of years earlier, however, Pope Gregory instructed his clergy to utilize pagan temples and buildings as Christian places of

---

[14] Ellerbe, Helen. *The Dark Side of Christian History.* Orlando: Morningstar and Lark 1995, 56. This belief may very well have been true.
[15] Benton, 1997, op cit., 23.

13

worship, to replace the pagan idols with Christian relics, to continue animal sacrifice but to use the meat for Christian feasts, and to keep some festivals and icons that had been popular with the peasants as aids to conversion and to increase church attendance. Reasons for the appearance of gargoyles and grotesques are many and they all may have some basis in fact.

The fact that gargoyles and grotesques continued in their popularity long after Christianity had pushed the pagan traditions aside attests to the images becoming cultural and architectural icons—decorative motifs in the best sense of the word—on secular as well as ecclesiastical structures.

While there is some debate as to the geographic origin of the grotesque, Goodyear wrote "The introduction of grotesque forms of animals or men in these ornaments is peculiar to [the Romanesque] period...These grotesques represent the fantastic and original spirit of the Germanic North as contrasted with the more sedate Byzantine dependence on earlier classic designs." [16]

Grundy discounts the assumption that the carvings were Christian symbols of evil and sin, writing, "taking into account St. Bernard's unfamiliarity with the carved imagery, it can...be anticipated that the subject-matter had little to do with Christian doctrine but much to do with the carvers themselves." [17] Anthony Weir and James Jerman provide us with another view though, "sculptures then, as workers now, did not carve what they were not commissioned to do, nor what they were not paid for." [18] In fact, according to these two researchers, "no mason would have been allowed to perpetrate, or been paid for, work of this kind in so exposed a position at the entrance to a Christian edifice, unless his work had been done with the connivance or direction of his patrons."[19]

---

[16] Goodyear, W.H. *Roman and Medieval Art.* Meadville: The Chautaugua-Century Press 1893, 155.
[17] Grundy, Thirlie. *Going in Search of the Green Man in Cumbria.* Cumbria: Thumbprint 2000, 6.
[18] Weir, Anthony and James Jerman. *Images of Lust: Sexual Carvings on Medieval Churches.* London: Routledge 1999, 8.
[19] Ibid., 20.

The carvings produced by these craftsmen undoubtedly reflect their own experiences, values, traditions and beliefs even though they were paid to carve them by an institution which must have viewed their work as reflective of Hell rather than heaven.

Master masons in the Middle Ages were not chosen at random. Rather, as Benton noted, they were required to undergo years of study in a church or monastery school, serve as an apprentice for another five to seven years, and then to create a "master work" which permitted them to become an "architect" of that period in time. [20] Each of the gargoyle and grotesque carvers worked closely with the master mason, who was responsible for the entire construction of the church or cathedral. The twentieth century stonemasons responsible for the gargoyles and grotesques present on the Washington National Cathedral are not so different as their 12th century brothers. "Wrought from personal experience and handcrafted with the tools and skills of their trade," notes folklorist Marjorie Hunt, "the stone carvers' freehand carvings are quintessential expressions of the spirit of freedom and responsibility that pervades their work—poignant, powerful statements of individual creativity and shared cultural values." [21] Stone carvers today, as they did in the past, share "esoteric" knowledge among themselves, knowledge which surfaces in their carvings.

"What they [the carvers] themselves thought of what they were doing, they did not tell us; they worked with stone, not words", wrote John Blackwood. "Perhaps they were just enjoying themselves." [22]

C.J.P. Cave believed that the many carvings appearing on churches during the Middle Ages were a mixture of Church direction and artisan choice. "The master builder," he wrote "may have been responsible for them, or the individual craftsmen may have made their own choice. ...there is no question that a programme fixed by church authorities would not have allowed the

---

[20] Benton 2002, 198
[21] Hunt, Marjorie. *The Stone Carvers: Master Craftsmen of Washington National Cathedral.* Washington: Smithsonian Institution Press 1999, 136.
[22] Blackwood, John. *Oxford's Gargoyles and Grotesques.* Oxford: Charon Press 1986, 2.

indecent little scenes found in some church bosses...." [23] However, he also noted that "in certain churches the subjects...were obviously chosen by the authorities, and the carvers had to follow their instructions...." [24] The give and take relationship of the cravers and their religious employers must have been agreeable to both, since the beautiful churches and cathedrals, adorned with gargoyles and grotesques, multiplied throughout Britain and Europe over the next few hundred years.

Nineteenth century historian W. H. Goodyear agreed, writing, "The stonecutter of the Middle Ages was given a capital to decorate and was himself the artist who conceived and did the whole thing. This means that the execution was vital and vigorous, that the pattern itself was an inventive and creative effort, not a mechanical copy..."[25] Goodyear also notes that each gargoyle was its own distinctive design—no two ever alike.

It is probable that many of the gargoyles found in churches were, in fact, intended as religious symbols—symbols of warning to a sinful population. Bridaham agreed, writing, "the clergy regarded every stone in the fabric of the cathedral as a religious symbol..." [26] Bridaham believed that the true meaning behind these sculptures is obscure today simply "because we have lost the unrecorded local tradition."[27]

"A gargoyle said to depict the devil devouring an unbaptized child on the south transept on the Church of Saint Aldhelm, in Doulton, England, supports this interpretation", [28] wrote Benton. A series of carvings at the Cathedral of Saint John in Den Bosch, the Netherlands graphically depicts people cringing in terror as gargoyles leap out from buttresses. This image, however, is unique to this 16th century cathedral.

---

[23] Cave, C.J.P. *Medieval Carvings in Exeter Cathedral.* London: Penguin Books 1953, 18.
[24] Ibid.
[25] Goodyear, op cit., 193.
[26] Bridaham, Lester Burbank. *Gargoyles, Chimeres, and The Grotesque in French Gothic Sculpture.* New York: Architectural Book Publishing Co., Inc. 1930, xii.
[27] Ibid.
[28] Benton, 1997, op cit., 24.

A fanged grotesque 923 7th Street. [29]

Many grotesques carved after the Middle Ages were undoubtedly created as decorative or for some other reason. The satyr sculptures appearing on the Wall Pavilion at The Zwinger in Dresden, crafted in the 1730's, were designed to offer some esoteric protection of the exotic plants there during the winter.

Dragons seem to fill everyone's dreams of fantasy. Children and adults both love them and they are important cultural icons in both the East and the West. They are also among the most common of those carvings known as "grotesques" and gargoyles. "Fantastic animals such as dragons," writes Rosa Giorgi, "became major figures in the history of art thanks to their being mentioned in canonical sources and legends..." [30]

[29] This grotesque adorns the front of the Sullivan Building, constructed 1857-58 at 923 7th Street.
[30] Giorgi, Rosa. *Angels and Demons in Art.* Los Angeles: The J. Paul Getty Museum 2005,

The dragon was often used to represent the Devil and evil. In legend, once the dragon (Devil) was defeated the entire population of pagans would convert to Christianity. Many early saints and martyrs are remembered for their heroic battles against terrible dragons in battles of good against evil. [31] And, of course, the saints won out in the end.

"There are no doubts about the negative qualities of the dragon," writes Belcari. The use of the dragon in religious iconography was obvious, "A mentality which was susceptible to magic beliefs and rituals gave rise to a defensive stance, and to convey its message, the church would often avail of the creatures of the popular imagination, which were recorded in contemporary bestiaries." [32]

However, the dragon is also the national symbol of Wales, appearing as the primary image on the Welsh flag. The Welsh Celts adopted the image, according to Alexander, "after Merlin found two dragons fighting each other in a cavern beneath Vortigern's fortress." [33] We must remember too that King Arthur's father was Uther Pendragon, whose name meant "Great Dragon." In China, the dragon represents the highest spiritual power as well as strength and supernatural wisdom. Again, as with most cultural symbols, its meaning is dual—representing both good and evil. The dragon was symbolic of the emperor's powers and role in mediating between heaven and earth. The Chinese believed that they were ancestors of the Yellow Emperor who reportedly had the head of a man and the body of a dragon.

Because the dragon symbolizes ferocity in battle, it often was adopted in heraldic crests throughout Europe—an obvious diversion from Church symbolism.

99.

[31] Some of these are, of course, St. George, the Archangel Michael, Saint Martha and Mary Magdalene who was said to have defeated a dragon with a blessing and a sprinkling of holy water.

[32] Belcari, Riccardo and Giulia Marrucchi. *Art of the Middle Ages.* Firenze: SCALA Group, S.p.A. 2007, 287.

[33] Alexander, Marc. *A Companion to the Folklore, Myths & Customs of Britain.* Phoenix Mill: Sutton Publishing Limited 2002, 73.

Kathleen Basford believed that the Green Man image found on so many cathedrals and other ecclesiastical structures represented punishment rather than life. Writing in her book *The Green Man*, she noted, "although the Green Man was a much loved motif I think it is very unlikely that he was revered as a symbol of the renewal of life in springtime." [34]

The Green Man, according to Basford, "represents the darkness of unredeemed nature" and "the root of all evil." [35] While the Green Man does have a dual nature, it is certainly not evil but illustrates the very characteristics of nature—both of death and life and mankind's fate if it chooses to abuse nature rather than live within the bounds of nature's rules. It appears more likely that those with strict Christian upbringing may see the "darkness and unredeemed nature" of the Green Man as perceived by Basford rather than as a representation of Nature and the spirit of the forests. It is perhaps our concept of "God" and "good and evil" which dictates for each of us what the Green Man is.

Marc Alexander wrote "The most puzzling aspect of the woodland entity known as the Green Man is that while he is obviously pagan, carvings of his face with foliage sprouting from his mouth are to be found in over a hundred cathedrals and churches in Britain...there is no explanation as to why representations of the Green Man were so universal." [36] Rosslyn Chapel, in Scotland, alone has over 100 Green Man images carved in stone.

[34] Basford, Kathleen. *The Green Man*. Cambridge: D.S. Brewer 1978, 20.
[35] Ibid., 21.
[36] Alexander, op cit. 114.

Terra cotta Green Man,[37] **ca. 1850 "Old Town"**

In North America, the carvings of Green Men are not part of religious architectural motifs, but rather incorporated into old public buildings such as post offices, banks and apartment buildings. This is contrary to those carvings in Britain where a majority, but not all, are found on, and in, church buildings. During the Middle Ages, as well as before this time, the buildings that were designed and built to last were places of power—those being castles and fortresses of the government and churches. We are familiar with many of the grotesque figures of gargoyles found on many of the cathedrals. So too do carvings of Green Men appear on and in these magnificent structures. The reasons for their appearance on these Christian shrines have been debated for years. They are considered by many to be pagan survivals, which were either incorporated by the early church architects to show dominance over pagan beliefs or intentionally carved by pagan stonemasons as an intended statement of "we are not vanquished." Some have suggested that the numerous carved foliate heads found in churches represent the continuation of the ancient Celtic head cult into the Christian era. [38] At the same

---

[37] The photo above is that of a terra cotta Green Man located on the Newton Booth home and store at 1015-17 Front Street in Old Town. Booth was California's eleventh governor (1871-73) and served as a US Senator as well from 1873-1879. He opened a wholesale grocery business at this location in 1850.

[38] As Janet and Colin Bord wrote in their book, *Earth Rites: Fertility Practices in Pre-Industrial Britain* (London: Granada Publishing Limited, 1982, 87), the foliated head "is so widespread a theme that no complete a list of British carvings has been, or could be,

time, other researchers suggest that the Green Man motif was popular simply as a survival of classical art and constitute a fondness of *style* rather than *substance of meaning*.[39]

The origin for the Green Man is surely ancient although its meaning may have changed and evolved over time. Malcolm Jones notes that "heads emerging from or above stylized acanthus leaves can be found in Roman sculpture (an on the third-century BCE so-called Jupiter columns at Cirencester and elsewhere." [40] Jones, however, believes that the foliate head was simply a "decorative commonplace" by the eighth century. [41]

Researcher Clive Hicks wrote, "Commentators have found no mention of the Green Man in Medieval texts, [42] and the image seems to have been used in a wholly intuitive way, accepted but not explained." [43] While many of the carvings, according to Hicks, were intended to be purely decorative, he also believes that a great many were the result "of a deep, but probably intuitive, sense of symbolism." [44] Researcher Carol Ballard has a similar view, writing in her booklet *The Green Man: The Shakespeare Connection:*

"...rarely, if ever, can the Green Man be said to be a purely decorative ornament devoid of meaning." [45]

---

compiled. They are likely to be seen in any church with pre-1500 features...". The Bords note (page 90) that these foliated heads, or Green Men", "suggest strongly to us that the vital force responsible for the continuance of all life was being depicted" and "to look at them is to be reminded of the earth's never-failing energy which year after year ensures that life continues to flourish".

[39] MacDermott, Mercia. *Explore Green Men.* Loughborough: Explore Books/Heart of Albion Press 2003.

[40] Jones, Malcolm. "Green Man" in *Medieval Folklore.* Oxford: Oxford University Press 2002, 186.

[41] Ibid.

[42] While the Green Men may not have been written about specifically in early texts, their images were used in illuminated manuscripts in the 10th century.

[43] Hicks, Clive. *The Green Man: A Field Guide.* Helhoughton: COMPASSbooks 2000, 8-9. Hicks' statement is true as far as specific commentaries written during that time, however, there are some manuscripts from this time that included the motif in the illustrations and the 13th century sketchbook of Villard de Honnecourt included several such depictions.

[44] Ibid. 9

[45] Ballard, Carol. *The Geen Man: The Shakespeare Connection.* Warwickshire: Self published 1999, 6

Basford agreed, proclaiming "Rarely if ever can the Green Man be considered a 'meaningless' ornament or an empty echo."[46]

There is also some indication that in the Christian church the Green Man is directly related to the Madonna and Child and to Jesus in particular. Hicks noted in his book, *The Green Man: A Field Guide,* that "one boss in the vault of the Lady Chapel in Ely might be seen as a green Virgin and Child, and another, at Lincoln, as a green Christ. Two of the most important we discovered were from Exeter Cathedral, where a choir corbel shows the Madonna and Child surrounded by the foliage pouring from the mouth of a Green Man, and from Frieburg im Breisgau, where the Easter Sepulcher, containing a carved figure of Christ in the tomb, is framed by weeping green men." According to Hicks, "these were clearly intentional iconography, not customary decoration, not pagan survivals, not warnings against sin."

However, C.J.P. Cave, a celebrated architectural photographer of British cathedrals, wrote "In various parts of the cathedral [of Exeter] we find heads with stems of plants coming out of their mouths. This motif is very common from Norman times to the end of the Gothic period, and I suppose that it may be a survival from tree worship which had come down through the Middle Ages, just as Jack-in-the-Green has come down almost to our own days." [47]

Nicholas Mann, writing in *His Story: Masculinity in the Post-Patriarchal World,* notes that it may seem ironic that the Green Man, a very pagan symbol, "makes his most frequent appearances in ecclesiastical architecture." However, Mann believes that "in this case, the denial of a chthonic and daemonic immanent power by the Church…has led to its most vital expression in the elements of wood and stone which form the places of worship of the Church. There is irony in this, a quality much loved by the Green Man." [48]

When did the carvings of the Green Men first appear in British ecclesiastical architecture? The evidence is that they first appeared

[46] Basford, Kathleen. *The Green Man.* Cambridge: D.S. Brewer 1978, 21
[47] Cave, C.J.P. *Medieval Carvings in Exeter Cathedral.* London: Penguin Books 1953, 12
[48] Mann, Nicholas R. *His Story: Masculinity in the Post-Patriarchal World.* St. Paul: Llewellyn Publications 1995, 143

in large numbers in the late Norman period, from the late 12th to the early 16th centuries.[49] This is the same period of time that gargoyles became prolifically crafted upon Europe's cathedrals. The Doel's note that the popularity of foliate head carvings was most evident in the 14th and 15th centuries following the Black Death. This would certainly make sense with the symbolism of life and fertility being associated with the Green Man—an intuitive response to the grotesque death that killed over a third of the population in Europe. Basford writes that the "history and development of the Green Man in the Church can...be followed continuously from the fourth or fifth century. Though pagan in origin, the motif evolved within the Church and, during the Middle Ages, became part of its symbolic language."[50]

The Green Man image was brought to Irish churches somewhere between 1128 and 1150 CE. Champneys wrote that the distinction between Norman influences on church architectural motifs and influences from other sources are difficult to determine, however "the human heads, sometimes of a grotesque kind, seem to...be of very early date...of unmistakably Norman character..."[51]

The Green Man may be identified more directly with Sylvanus, the Roman "country god', the god of the oak. Thirlie Grundy, writing in her little book *The Green Man in Northumberland and County Durham*, notes that during the Middle Ages when the large stone churches began to replace the small wooden ones, stonemasons did not exist. It was the wood carvers who were called upon to fashion the extensive and ornate stonework. "On finding themselves in charge of stone-building projects", asserts Grundy, the woodcarvers "had summoned the aid of their most trustworthy ally—the powerful, spiritual god of the oak, or today's enigmatic Green Man." [52] Sylvanus, also known as the "woodland god", was a

---

[49] Doel, Fran & Geoff. *The Green Man in Britain*. Gloucestershire: Tempus Publishing Ltd. 2001, 37

[50] Basford 1978, op cit., 19

[51] Champneys, Arthur C. *Irish Ecclesiastical Architecture*. New York: Hacker Art Books/Irish University Press 1970, 114-115

[52] Grundy, Thirlie. *The Green Man in Northumberland and County Durham*. Carlisle Cumbria: Thumbprint 2001, 3

Roman-Celtic tree deity of ancient Britain. Basford wrote of a leaf mask carving on a fountain at the French Abbey of Saint-Denis. Dating back to 1200 CE the fountain has a series of heads carved on the basin, each head with the name of a particular deity engraved over it. The one Green Man face represented is named "Silvan."[53] An altar dedicated to him was set up in Yorkshire, on Scargill Moor, by the occupying Roman army. [54]

The concept of the woodland god, the foliate head or Green Man, appears to have followed the Roman armies as they trekked through conquered lands, eventually adopted by the early Christians who aided in the Green Man's spread along trade and pilgrim routes. While early Christian authorities may have used the Green Man image to induce the pagan community to go to church, it is also possible that the early Christian faith did not have a clear definition between the ancient Pagan traditions and the new Christian faith, which so heavily borrowed from the past. Because of this lack of definition, the two traditions became fused together—pagan and Christian—co-existing in the same religious structures for hundreds of years. As researcher John Timpson wrote, "maybe in those days no one was quite sure they [the pagan gods] wouldn't make a comeback—so these medieval craftsmen were just hedging their bets." [55]

William Anderson, however, believed that the incorporation of the Green Man motif into church architecture and art was perhaps unconsciously intentional:

"...the missionary saints needed to bring the greatest source of living power on earth under the guidance of Christ: the power that is in grass and leaf and sap on which all living things depend. Though they knew that demonic forces dwelt among the works of Nature, they had at the same time to assert the goodness of creation, and there arose a dualism between their fear of the demonic and the

[53] Basford 1978, op.cit. 15
[54] Hutton, Ronald. *The Pagan Religions of the Ancient British Isles: Their Nature and Legacy.* Oxford: Blackwell Publishers Ltd 1991, 208
[55] Timpson, John. *Timpson's Leylines: A Layman Tracking the Ley's.* London: Cassell & Co. 2000, 29

beauty and usefulness of God's work." [56] Green Man researcher Mike Harding has estimated that there are five times the numbers of Green Man figures in Exeter Cathedral as there are of Jesus. This would certainly imply that they have held an important function and spiritual place in the Christian church for a significant period of time prior to the Reformation.

One notable boss at Exeter is that of a woman within a mass of vines, holding the stems in her hands. Cave believed that many of these carvings were not completed under Church authority, but rather by craftsmen that "may in such bosses easily have given rein to their humour, knowing that as soon as the work was done it would pass unnoticed from the floor of the church...." [57] Other images that may be thought strange in Christian churches, unless one takes into account the then contemporary mixture of folk-religion, paganism and Christianity, include wild men and centaurs. Cave notes that early legend "explains the human part of the centaur as a type of Christ." [58]

The early Church's obvious comfort with pagan imagery is most noticeable on the tomb of Saint Abre in the Church of Saint-Hilaire-le-Grand in Poitiers. The tomb, dating from the 4th or 5 century C.E., is decorated with a variety of Pagan themes, including dolphins, and a foliate head. Basford notes, "it is a curious carving, quite unlike the Hellenistic leaf masks. The head is surrounded by contiguous and overlapping leaves which may represent the hair and beard, while large sprays of stylized foliage and flowers spring from the nostrils and extend on either side of the head, like fantastic moustaches." [59] It is this carving, according to Basford, which may be the prototype of the Green Man images of the medieval period. The foliate head at Saint Abre is the first example of the "disgorger

---

[56] Anderson, William. *Green Man: The Archetype of our Oneness with the Earth*. London: Harper Collins 1990, 54.
[57] Cave, op cit., 18

[58] Ibid, 22
[59] Basford, K. H. "Quest for the Green Man", in *Symbols of Power*. Edited by H.R. Ellis Davidson. Cambridge: D.S. Brewer Ltd. 1977, 107

of vegetation" in Europe. [60] It was from this same area in France that the Gothic style of Green Man developed. [61]

For approximately three hundred years, between the 10th and 12th centuries, the foliate mask began to change, to represent evil and sin—in fact; the foliate head became part of the exclusive realm of demonology. To this day, many examples of these demon masks exist—including some in the United States. The 13th century reversed this trend with a delightful focus on the lifelike and natural quality of the carved leaves. The obvious struggle between nature and man is shown in many of the Green Man images during the 13th to 15th centuries.

Sexuality and fertility may be associated with the Green Man image in some areas. Weir and Jerman believe that some Green Men were carved by craftsmen that had the May Day festivals in mind rather than anything else. "At Linley in Shropshire," they write, "a twelfth-century weather-worn tympanum depicts a figure, arms akimbo, legs widely-splayed, surrounded by greenery, some of which sprouts from him." [62]

Myth and images of the Green Man certainly influenced the art of the Florentine Renaissance.[63] Fifteenth century artist Sandro Botticelli (1444-1510), who painted for the Medici family for half of his life, was given artistic freedom by Lorenzo Medici who was himself influenced by Christian Neo-Platonism, which tried to reconcile classical (pagan) and Christian views. Botticelli's *La Primavera,* painted around 1478, is perhaps his most famous painting incorporating Pagan themes in the Christian Neo-platonism philosophy. However, *La Primavera,* like Botticelli's *Birth of Venus,* has remained somewhat a mystery. According to Jean Seznec, "their ultimate secret has not yet been penetrated—or rather,

---

[60] Anderson, William. op cit. 46

[61] Harte, Jeremy. *The Green Man.* Andover: Pitkin Unichrome Ltd 2001, 2

[62] Weir, Anthony and James Jerman. *Images of Lust: Sexual Carvings on Medieval Churches.* London: Routledge 1999, 148.

[63] Likewise, "Christian literature in…learned language was permeated by the allusions, thought, symbolism, mythology, and esthetic of the pagan past, inevitably" notes Ramsay MacMullen in his book *Christianity & Paganism in the Fourth to Eighth Centuries,* pg. 147. It is not difficult to see how easily art was also influenced by these "pagan" qualities.

their secrets, for it is our belief that they hide several layers of allegorical meaning." [64]

The most striking aspect of *La Primavera*, a painting depicting Venus attended by Mercury, the Three Graces, Flora, Cupid and others, is the appearance of a flowering vine flowing from the mouth of a wood nymph. According to Robert Coughlan, this painting is an allegory of spring that "takes place on a flowered plain, backed by a forest where trees bloom and bear fruit at the same time." [65] Even though the painting, while appearing pagan in theme, "is a Christian painting" [66] reflecting the Neo-Platonist philosophy of the time, this would be one of the last paintings to incorporate the symbiotic themes of Nature and humans being linked physically together. The vine gushing from the Nymphs mouth surely was inspired by the foliate masks found around Botticelli's environment and it struck a cord with him. Nowhere could a finer example of the meaning of rebirth and regeneration be found than in such a depiction.

With the overthrow of the Medici court by French armies things changed. The arrival of the Dominican monk Savonarola sealed the fate of Botticelli's artistic freedom. It was "the reforming priest-dictator", according to Helen Gardner's *Art Through the Ages,* "who denounced the paganism of the Medici and their artists, philosophers, and poets"[67] and who caused the decline of Florentine culture. Botticelli turned his talents to painting safer Christian subjects.

Some foliate heads were the work of Michelangelo, appearing on the tombs of Pope Julius II in Rome and on the Medici Chapel in Florence. Many historical figures in Britain have Green Man images as part of their tombs dating back to the Renaissance and, in fact, it

---

[64] Seznec, Jean. *The Survival of the Pagan Gods: The Mythological Tradition and Its Place in Renaissance Humanism and Art.* New York: Harper Torchbooks/The Bollingen Library 1961,112.

[65] Coughlan, Robert. *The World of Michelangelo 1475-1564.* New York: Time-Life Books 1966, 53.

[66] Ibid.

[67] Gardner, Helen. *Art Through the Ages, Fifth Edition.* New York: Harcourt, Brace & World, Inc. 1970, 443.

may be due to the influence of the Renaissance that finally got the Green Man out of the church and into secular architecture. Along with the forced insistence of Reformation leaders, that classic religious imagery no longer had a place in ecclesiastical buildings. An ivory helmet owned by George II (1722-60) is decorated with a foliate mask on each side, along with the Royal Coat of Arms and a winged dragon. It would seem that, to the King, the foliate mask was symbolic of power as well as of rebirth and renewal.

It appears that this struggle, at least as shown in contemporary Green Man art, has changed to one of a symbiotic relationship between humankind and nature. The foliate head has given birth to such garden ornaments as leafy children, birdbaths and other items, which embrace life and the spirits of nature.

The artisans employed to construct and decorate the early churches were, says Grundy, "chosen for their skills rather than for their Christian beliefs." [68] "On finding themselves in charge of stone-building projects" Grundy writes, "…they had summoned the aid of their most trustworthy ally—the powerful, spiritual god of the oak, or today's enigmatic Green Man." [69] We must be thankful to the Church for the survival of the Green Man image into the 21st century.

I believe that it is of interest that in a few instances the Green Man appears in very close proximity to Christian churches. In California, a series of Green Man sculptures appears on an apartment building built around 1914 that is directly diagonal to the Catholic Cathedral in Sacramento. Likewise, in San Luis Obispo two marvelous Green Men were artistically carved in a Carnegie Library built in 1905 and located across the street from Mission San Luis Obispo constructed in 1772. While not intentionally created simply because a large and historic Christian church was nearby, it almost appears that there was an unconscious intent to create something to balance the heavy Christian influence of these two

---

[68] Grundy, Thirlie. *Going in Search of the Green Man in Cumbria.* Cumbria: Thumbprint 2000, 5.
[69] Grundy, Thirlie. *The Green Man in Northumberland and County Durham.* Cumbria: Thumbprint 2001, 3.

locations.

Green Man, El Cortez Apartments, 1914.

Sacramento boasts a number of fine Green Man carvings including an apartment building at 1100 11th Street which has several different examples staring down on the pedestrian traffic below. The Green Man photographs shown on this and the following page were taken at that location. Built in 1914 the El Cortez Apartments, formerly the Howe Apartments, was home to several state legislators as it was a short distance from the Capitol building.

Green Men (ca.1914) located near the Sacramento Cathedral, 11th and K Street

One of the most ornate Green Man images I have ever seen in the United States or Great Britain is located over a Starbucks Coffee shop on 8th and K streets in Sacramento. Created in 1899, this horned Green Man looks on with an almost amused expression. The observer should note that horns represent supernatural power, divinity, virility, fertility and abundance. It is interesting that horned Green Men are more common in the United States than they are in the UK. Green Men are equated with renewal and rebirth.

Horned Green Man, 717 K Street street, Sacramento

Another unusual Green Man exhibiting a decidedly maritime theme can be found above the entryway to the Sacramento City Hall on I street.

City Hall Green Man

Several different types of Green Men adorn the Masonic Temple at 1123 J Street. Built in 1920 this structure not only has Green Men but two full sized figures of knights standing on both sides of the entry way. The architect of the Masonic Temple was Rudolph Herold who also designed City Hall (above) and Capital National Bank—both which have their own unique symbols.

The photos below depict the various Green Men on the outside of the Masonic Temple. The Masonic Temple is one of the last buildings in Sacramento to use the revivalist architectural styles.

Masonic Temple Green Man, 1920

Green Man and two other decorations outside the stained glass window of the Masonic Temple.

MERMAIDS

One of the most ancient, fascinating and erotic images that humans have conceived of is the mermaid. Made popular in the animated movie, *The Little Mermaid*, she has been an important figure in folklore and mythology since Babylon and is known in every culture from the Middle East to those of the North American Indians. She also shows up in church architecture.

Stories about mermen and mermaids can be traced back to ancient Babylonian mythology, from the Old Babylonian times onward through the history of Mesopotamia and into the modern world. In fact, as Richard Carrington so aptly put it, "There is not an age, and hardly a country in the world, whose folklore does not contain some reference to mermaids or to mermaid-like creatures. They have been alleged to appear in a hundred different places, ranging from the mist-covered shores of Norway and Newfoundland to the palm-studded islands of the tropic seas." [70]

The Babylonian god Oannes, a half-man half-fish deity, has been depicted on ancient sculptures dating back at least to 2000 BCE. Like all mermen, he is shown with the body of a man but from the waist down, he is in the form of a fish. Oannes taught the Babylonians the arts, sciences and letters and possessed vast knowledge.

"To the Assyrians," wrote Jeremy Black and Anthony Green, "the creature was known simply as kulullû, 'fish-man'…representations of these figures were used in Neo-Assyrian art for the purpose of protective nature…" [71] This "fish-man", wrote Black and Green, "is perhaps the prototype for the merman figure in Greek and Medieval European art and literary tradition."[72] The

[70] Carrington, Richard. *Mermaids and Mastodons: A Book of Natural & Unnatural History.* New York: Rinehart & Company, Inc. 1957, 5.
[71] Black, Jeremy &Anthony Green. *Gods, Demons and Symbols of Ancient Mesopotamia.* Austin: University of Texas Press 1992, 131-132.

kulullû obviously was an important mystical symbol for the Babylonians as priests were often garbed in the fish-man guise as part of healing rituals.

Double-tailed Romanesque Mermaid at St. Die Cathedral (France), 11ᵗʰ century. [73]

Vishnu, one of the most venerated and sophisticated deities of the Hindu pantheon, known as the "preserver and restorer," is depicted at times as a man-fish. One of his forms is that of Matsya, the Fish, which saved humankind from the Flood. According to traditional lore, Vishnu, in the form of a fish, told King Manu that a flood would occur in seven days. He told the king to build a boat and to ensure that the seven sages, or hermits, were on board along with seeds of all plants and one animal of each species. When the boat was finished and loaded the fish (Vishnu) told the king to tie

[72] Ibid, 131.
[73] From *Gargoyles, Chimeres, and the Grotesque in French Gothic Sculpture.* New York: Architectural Book Publishing Company, Inc. 1930 by Lester Burbank Bridaham.

the boat to the fish. The king used the royal serpent Vasuki as a rope and tied the boat to the back of the giant fish. The fish then towed the boat to Mt. Himavan until the flood waters reseeded. The world was then repopulated with plants, animals and humankind. Matsya is Vishnu's first incarnation as a protector and preserver of the world.

Folklorist Horace Beck wrote "it is my belief that what we are dealing with when discussing...mermaids is really a fractured mythology—beliefs so old as possibly to reach back to Neolithic times, beliefs long since vanished into limbo, with only fragments remaining."[74] Beck believes that the core myths of the mermaids have a northern European origin but I believe that they have a common origin that was "hard wired" in our minds as a species and not as geographical mythology. It would seem that a common religious and cultural tradition existed at one time in our ancient history; a tradition that still surfaces now and then in our mythology and folklore. Like the Fairy, the legend of the mermaids may also come from this tradition.

Mythic stories of mermaids, nymphs and water spirits may be survival tales of the sea Goddesses. Through time, the original stories became more and more elaborate and took on a flavor of their own from the people who passed the stories on. Folklorist Shahrukh Husain, in her book The Goddess, wrote, "the sea goddess survives in a debased form as water-sprites, sirens or mermaids. Probably the first mermaids were images of the fish-tailed Aphrodite—they are famously able to seduce men away from the land, and draw them down to their underwater kingdom. A reminder of their lost divinity lies in the tales of a mermaid....receiving the souls of drowned men." [75]

Part of the fascination we have with Mermaids is not only their beauty, but also the danger associated with them. In fact, according to Joseph Campbell, the mermaid image reflects the life threatening as well as the life-furthering aspects of water.[76] Legends of sailors

---

[74] Beck, Horace. *Folklore and the Sea.* Mystic: Mystic Seaport Museum Incorporated 1973, 266.

[75] Husain, Shahrukh. *The Goddess.* Alexandria: Time-Life Books 1997, 51.

[76] Campbell, Joseph. *The Masks of God: Primitive Mythology.* New York: The Viking

capturing these creatures for a short time or living with them longer as husband and wife are interspersed with other stories with more dire results. Fiske noted, "it has been a common superstition among sailors, that the appearance of a mermaid, with her hair comb and looking-glass, foretokens shipwreck, with the loss of all on board."[77]

Native Americans possess many legends of River Mermaids. The ancient Greeks had Eurynome, who was said to be the daughter of the God Oceanus. Eurynome was "a woman down to the buttocks and below that like a fish."[78] Of Eurynome Brewster wrote she "was most probably a local river nymph with the body like a mermaid's."[79]

In African (Benin) folklore the River Goddess Igbaghon ruled the underworld, which was under the waters surface. She was waited upon by mermaids who informed her of trespassers who went to the river to wash or to fetch water—they never returned from their tasks.[80]

South African anthropologist Penny Bernard, who has studied water spirit lore and traditions in that part of the world, has found that many of the traits of the Native American river mermaids also exist in South African tribal beliefs. These water spirits are referred to as the "River People" and are believed to live in certain deep pools of water, especially below waterfalls. Bernard notes, "some informants say they are fair skinned, with long dark hair, are naked and some have half-human, half-fish physical attributes (mermaid like)." [81] She also reports that these creatures only live in "living water"—that is, water that is flowing in rivers, the ocean or waterfalls. Some, however, are also reported to reside in wells in

Press 1959, 62.

[77] Fiske, John. *Myths and Myth-Makers: Old Tales and Superstitions Interpreted by Comparative Mythology.* Boston: Houghton, Mifflin and Company 1881, 103.

[78] Brewster, Harry. *The River Gods of Greece: Myths and Mountain Waters in the Hellenic World.* London: I.B. Tauris & Co. Ltd. 1997, 97.

[79] Ibid.

[80] Osoba, Funmi. *Benin Folklore: A Collection of Classic Folktales and Legends.* London: Hadada Books 1993, 40.

[81] Bernard, Penny. "Mermaids, Snakes and the Spirits of the Water in Southern Africa: Implications for River Health", lecture given in *Shortcourse on the Role and Use of Aquatic Biomonitoring.* Rhodes University, Grahamstown, South Africa, 2000.

Zimbabwe. Normally this tradition is found only in the more arid areas of Africa.

Double-tailed merman, Sutter Club[82]

Water spirits as well cannot simply be dismissed as metaphors. The almost universal application of human-like characteristics and supra-natural powers, like those of the Fairies, demands a broader approach. At least through the 19th century the people of Christian

---

[82] This sculpture is located near the entry of Sacramento's Sutter Club. Originally founded in January 1889 the present building was completed in 1930. Members of the club included gold miners, legislators and many governors. This beautiful structure is located at 1220 9th Street.

Norway left offerings to water spirits every Christmas Day. The following account appeared in the December 17, 1859 issue of the British journal, Notes & Queries:

"...a fisherman wished on Christmas Day to give the Spirit of the Waters a cake; but when he came to the shore, lo! the waters were frozen over. Unwilling to leave his offering upon the ice, and so to give the Spirit the trouble of breaking the ice to obtain it, the fisherman took a pickaxe, and set to work to break a hole in the ice. In spite of all his labour he was only able to make a very small hole, not nearly large enough for him to put the cake through. Having laid the cake on the ice, while he thought what was best to be done, suddenly a very tiny little hand as white as snow was stretched through the hole, which seizing the cake and crumpling it up together, withdrew with it. Ever since that time the cakes have been so small that the Water Spirits have had no trouble with them."

Mysterious water creatures have been reported throughout the world's folklore for hundreds and thousands of years. Like the Fairy, these creatures also have almost universal characteristics and descriptions. California Miwok Indians called these creatures He-Há-Pe, or "River Mermaids" and described them as "beautiful fish-women [that] had long black hair and lived in deep pools and rivers." [83] Other California tribes referred to these creatures as "Water Women" in their mythology. The "River Mermaids" reportedly pulled victims to their deaths in these deep waters.[84]

Nineteenth-century writer S. Baring-Gould reported several instances of the capture of supposed mer-people. One such instance was the capture of a "Marmennill" or merman off the Icelandic island of Grimsey in the early 14th century, one also reportedly washed up on the beaches of Suffolk in 1187.[85] Baring-Gould notes other cases as well of mermen not only being seen but caught in

[83] Varner, Gary R. *Sacred Wells: A Study in the History, Meaning, and Mythology of Holy Wells & Waters.* Baltimore: Publish America 2002, 129.
[84] Merriam, C. Hart. Editor. *The Dawn of the World: Myths and Tales of the Miwok Indians of California.* Lincoln: University of Nebraska Press 1993, pg. 228-230.
[85] Baring-Gould, S. *Curious Myths of the Middle Ages.* New York: John B. Alden, Publishers 1885, 205.

1305 and 1329 off Iceland, 1430 in Holland, 1531 in the Baltic, 1560 on an island west of Ceylon, and 1714 in the West Indies.

According to Baring-Gould, the 1560 incident occurred near the island of Mandar. It was here that "some fishermen entrapped in their net seven mermen and mermaids, of which several Jesuits, and Father Henriques, and Bosquez, physician to the Viceroy of Goa, were witnesses. The physician examined them with a great deal of care, and dissected them. He asserts that the internal and external structure resembled that of human beings." [86] Baring-Gould gives several other accounts of mer-folk being captured, and examined by sailors and other villagers from Ceylon, Holland and the Shetland Islands. Other reported sightings include one made by Henry Hudson's men on June 15, 1608, Captain Richard Whitbourne in 1620 at St. John's Harbor in Newfoundland, and Captain John Smith in 1614 in the West Indies. Even today, mermaids are commonly reported near the Isle of Man.

John C. Messenger, in his ethnography of a small Irish island he called Inis Beag, noted during his study that "At least one and maybe three mermaids are associated with particular locations along the coastline of the island. The spirit usually is found sitting on a rock with her tail in the water and combing her long hair, although she has been seen hovering over the surface of the sea in a 'robe of mist.'" [87]

Angelo Rappoport noted, "The sacred wells are a very favourite place with the fair children of the sea. Here, undisturbed by men, the green-haired beauties of the ocean lay aside their garb and revel in the clear moonlight." [88] There are very few sacred wells at the ocean however, and Rappaport does not say how they journey to these places.

In Zulu lore mermaids would, at times, possess mediums and give them healing powers. They were also believed to come out of

---

[86] Ibid, op cit., 227.

[87] Messenger, John C. *Inis Beag: Isle of Ireland.* Case Studies in Cultural Anthropology. New York: Holt, Rinehart and Winston 1969, 100.

[88] Rappoport, Angelo. *The Sea: Myths and Legends.* London: Senate 1995, 184. A reprint of the 1928 edition published by Stanley Paul & Company, London. Originally titled *Superstitions of Sailors.*

the waters at night, causing humans to avoid rivers and the ocean after nightfall.

Among both American Indian and African beliefs is that the River Mermaids and the River People must be treated with respect and fear—for both of these creatures would often lure unsuspecting individuals to their deaths or to live the remainder of their lives under water. This fear is universal among the world's indigenous peoples. Among the Udmurt people of Estonia, water spirits would drown those humans who swam at the wrong time or swam without wearing a crucifix. [89]

Russia has its own tales of dangerous Water Spirits. "Water Grandfather," according to Joseph Campbell, "is an adroit shapeshifter and is said to drown people who swim at midnight or at noon." [90] Like the beautiful Mermaid, this shapeshifter likes to sit in the moonlight and comb his long green hair and beard. He is not above asking humans for help however. He often seeks out a village midwife when one of his wives is about to deliver a baby and she is paid handsomely in gold and silver.

There are, indeed, many similarities among the African water deities-mermaids and those of other parts of the world. All seem to possess beautiful long hair, combs, mirrors and very fair skin. Other explanations for such tales may be the sighting of unexpected but perfectly natural animals appearing in many of the eerie water locations around the world. Would the flash of a large fish in a "spooky" lake be misinterpreted as a mermaid? Perhaps. But can such an event explain the mermaid tales from other areas that did not have the same exposure to such primal cultural symbols?

The Pascagoula Indians of Louisiana not only respected the mermaid—they worshipped one. According to E. Randall Floyd, "legend has it that an entire...tribe—the Biloxi, also known as the Pascagoula—marched into a raging river at the command of a mermaid-like sea-goddess and drowned." [91] This happened,

---

[89] Lintrop, Aado. "On the Udmurt Water Spirit and the Formation of the Concept 'Holy" Among Permian Peoples" in Folklore, Vol. 26, April 2004, 9. Published by the Folk Belief & Media Group of the Estonian Literary Museum, Tartu.
[90] Campbell, Joseph. *The Hero With a Thousand Faces.* New York: MJF Books 1949, 80.

according to legend, in the 1500's. It was said that within a week after a white priest journeyed to the tribe, commanding them to "abandon their superstitions in an underwater goddess", they disappeared in the waters of the Pascagoula River.

Some Native American lore states that a merman actually was responsible for their arrival on American shores. According to Rappoport, such a creature led the ancestors of modern Indians from Asia to America when he took pity on them one day when they were suffering from hunger. "Following the fish-man" Rappoport wrote, "they ultimately reached the American coast."[92] The merman was described as having green hair and beard, a forked tail and a face shaped like a porpoise. This creature, according to Baring-Gould, appeared suddenly one day "in the season of opening buds."

"The people of our nation," so says the legend, "were much terrified at seeing a strange creature, much resembling a man, riding upon the waves. ...But if our people were frightened at seeing a man who could live in the water like a fish or a duck, how much more were they frightened when they saw that from his breast down he was actually a fish, or rather two fishes, for each of his legs was a whole and distinct fish." [93] Contemporary accounts of mermaid sightings read like daily news reports. Explorer Henry Hudson, on one of his attempts to open the Northwest Passage, wrote of one such event:

"This evening [June 15] one of our company, looking overboard, saw a mermaid, and, calling up some of the company to see her, one more of the crew came up, and by that time she was come close to the ship's side, looking earnestly on the men. A little after a sea came and overturned her. From the navel upward, her back and breasts were like a woman's, as they say that saw her; her body as big as one of us. Her skin very white, and long hair hanging down behind, of colour black. In her going down they saw her tail, which was like the tail of a porpoise, speckled like a mackerel." [94]

[91] Floyd, E. Randall. *Great Southern Mysteries*. Little Rock: August House Publishers 1989, 118.
[92] Rappoport, op cit., 165.
[93] Baring-Gould, op cit., 222.

Mermaids are also found in medieval church architectural ornament. However, she does not appear to be regarded as simply "ornamental," on the contrary the mermaid is "a symbol of the lure for mankind" to sin. [95] The mermaid gargoyle at Reims Cathedral in France, according to Bridaham, was a "Symbol of Enticements of the Flesh."[96] As Simpson and Roud wrote, the mermaid "was regarded as a natural if freakish creature, not a supernatural being....She made an excellent moral symbol for preachers, who identified her with the fatal attractions of wealth, sex, drink, etc. For this reason, mermaids are common in minor church sculpture; it is presumably as symbols of vanity that they acquired their comb and mirror, not known in classical art." [97]

Indeed, "the theme of luring men to disaster," wrote Weir and Jerman, "by sensual and sensory means was exactly the sort of thing that appealed to medieval moralizers." [98]

Carvings show the mermaid as both as single-tailed and double-tailed. While the single-tailed creature was regarded as symbolic of fornication by the church, the double-tailed creature was linked to "luxury" or lust—both being mortal sins.

Obviously, these characteristics were later attributes applied by Christianity for the mermaid's original meaning was far different. In Russia, mermaid figures were carved on wooden paddles used in washing clothes and were meant as protective rather than sexual symbols. Their long association as water goddesses cannot be denied.

Some scientists believe that sightings of mermaids are the result of seals, sea-cows and manatees seen from afar. However, it is not that simple to explain these ancient tales through scientific analysis. Anthropologist Richard Carrington wrote "...the natural history of mermaids cannot be understood by the methods of natural science

---

[94] As quoted by Richard Carrington in "The Natural History of the Mermaid", in Horizon, January, 1960, Vol. II, Number 3, 131.

[95] Cave, C.J.P. *Medieval Carvings in Exeter Cathedral.* London: Penguin Books 1953, 21.

[96] Bridaham, Lester Burbank. *Gargoyles, Chimeres, and the Grotesque in French Gothic Sculpture.* New York: Architectural Book Publishing Company, Inc. 1930, 11.

[97] Simpson and Roud, op cit., 234.

[98] Weir and Jerman, op cit., 49.

alone. These hauntingly beautiful goddesses of the sea, full of mystery and danger, were surely conjured from the chaos of the waters in answer to some primal human need. Their genus and species may not be carefully docketed in the Nomenclator Zoologicus, but their reality in terms of poetic truth is firmly established in the impassioned imagination of men." [99]

The existence of mermaids was certain to 17th century man. The 1688 issue of *Aberdeen Almanack, or New Prognostication for the Year 1688* read:

"To conclude for this year 1688. Near the place where the famous Dee payeth his Tribute to the German Ocean, *if curious Observers of wonderfull things in Nature*, will be pleased thither to resort, the 1, 13, and 29 of May; and on diverse other days in the ensuing Summer; as also in the Harvest tyme, to the 7 and 14 October, *they will undoubtedly see a pretty Company of MAR-MAIDS, creatures of admirable beauty*, and likewise hear their charming sweet Melodious Voices."

The photo on the following page shows a frightening sea-creature. Complete with a lobster tail, wings and a monstrous face, it is located just underneath the Green Man at the Newton Booth building. Who created this image from our dark fears? No doubt an artistisan familiar with sea-lore as this is just a few yards from the Sacramento River in Old Town Sacramento.

---

[99] Carrington, 1957 op cit. 19.

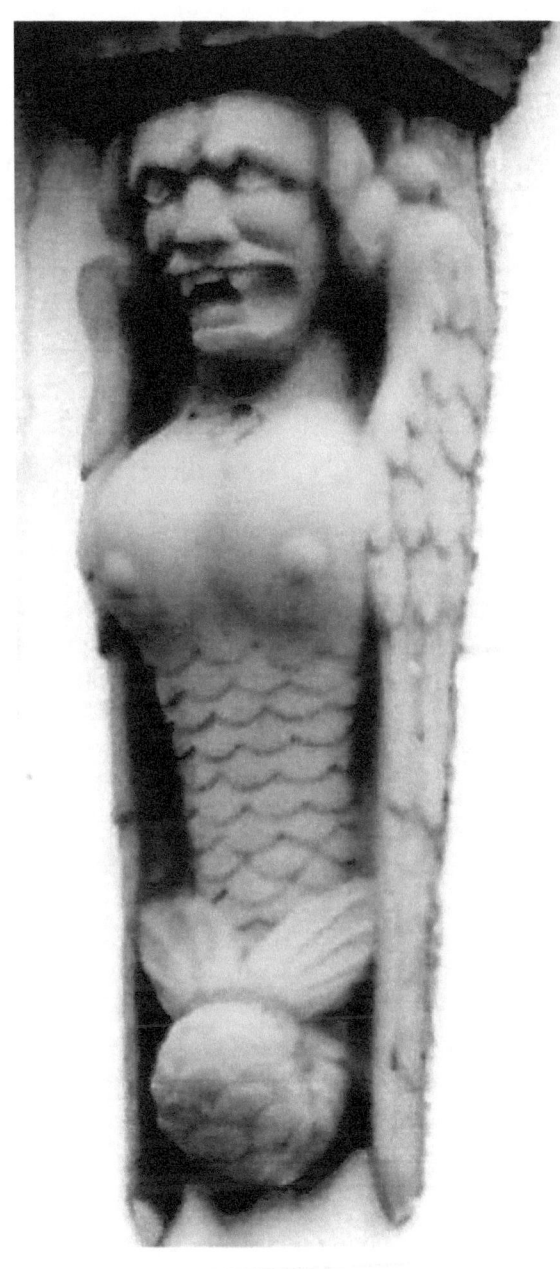

Old Town grotesque on the Newton Booth building, 1015-17 Front Street

45

A BESTIARY

Griffins, lions and unicorns abound as some of the images and decorative art that appears on our structures. All are important aspects of pagan mythology and meaning. Aniela Jaffe' wrote in *Man and his Symbols:*

"In the religions and religious art of practically every race, animal attributes are ascribed to the supreme gods, or the gods are represented as animals.

"The boundless profusion of animal symbolism in the religion and art of all times does not merely emphasize the importance of the symbol; it shows how vital it is for men to integrate into their lives the symbol's psychic content--instinct." [100]

Winged Lions and Griffins

The most common animal portrayed in the local architectural motifs is that of the lion. As Jaffe' indicated in the above work, "the elephant and the lion stand higher" [101] in the hierarchy of being than does man.

It is easy to see why the lion has evoked such sentiment among people as it has. It is a noble beast. Frazer wrote that the Namaquas people of Africa would not eat the flesh of a hare, as they believed that by doing so they, themselves, would become faint hearted. However, Frazer continues, "they eat the flesh of the lion, or drink the blood of the leopard or lion, to get courage and strength of these beasts."[102]

The lion is not only an important symbol to the Pagan. It also stands out in Christian theology. E.P. Evans notes that the lion "appears to have been a favorite symbol of the resurrection of Christ, as well as of the general resurrection..." [103]

---

[100] Jaffe', Aniela. "Symbolism in the Visual Arts", in *Man and His Symbols,* ed. by Carl G. Jung, New York: Doubleday & Company, 1964, 237

[101] Ibid, 238

[102] Frazer, Sir James. *The Golden Bough: A Study in Magic and Religion.* Hertfordshire: Wordsworth Editions 1993, 495.

[103] Evans, E.P. *Animal Symbolism in Ecclesiastical Architecture.* London: W. Heineman,

Evans continues to say, "the belief that the lion never closes its eyes in sleep caused this animal to be placed at the doors of churches as guardian of the sanctuary." [104] It is interesting to note that Evans also says that while this was a Christian practice, the ancient Egyptians also observed this belief--predating the Christian usage by thousands of years.

In fact, the lion was used extensively as a symbol of the sun god in Greece and Rome and was associated with the Goddess as well. The Goddesses Cybele, Astarte and Ishtar all have been depicted as riding upon lion or having lions pull their chariots. Campbell, in *The Masks of God: Primitive Mythology*, stated, "in India and the Near East the usual animal-mount of the goddess was the lion; in Egypt, Sekhmet was a lioness; and in the arts of both the Hittites and of the modern Yoruba of Nigeria the goddess stands poised on the lion, nursing her child." [105]

Donald Mackenzie wrote lions are "the guardians of the world deity" and that the seals of Crete "depict the mother goddess on a mountain-top supported similarly by a couple of lions, and also standing or seated between a lion and a lioness." Mackenzie theorized that the lion "was evidently the symbol of the earth, and the various figures of lions devouring animals, found in various countries, probably symbolized the earth receiving its propitiatory sacrifice."[106]

The lion shown on the next page adorns the National Gold Bank of D.O. Mills and Company which was built in 1912. This building is known as an impressive example of the Classical Revival style.

1896, 82.
[104] Ibid, 86.
[105] Campbell, Joseph. *The Masks of God: Primitive Mythology.* New York: Viking Press 1959, 330.
[106] Mackenzie, Donald A. *Crete & Pre-Hellenic Myths and Legends.* London: Senate 1995, 307.

A guardian lion peering down from a lofty Sacramento cornice, 631 J Street.

The lion has long been associated with potency and rulership. Saunders wrote in *Animal Spirits* that the lion, in Greek mythology, "represented the ravening power of death" [107] and was regarded as the guardian of the underworld in Egyptian mythology. According to William Olcott, the Egyptians also associated the lion with the sun due to, Olcott states, "by the fact that the Egyptians placed the figures of lions under the throne of Horus." [108] The lion was also representative of the sun by the ancient Sumerians. Olcott wrote that the lion was regarded as the solar symbol not only by the Egyptians, but by the Hindus, Chaldeans and Persians as well. He goes on to state that the Egyptian Osirian funeral rituals included the following prayer:

"Let me not be surpassed by the Lion god: Oh, the Lion of the Sun, who lifts his arm in the hill: I am the Lions, I am the sun. The white lion is the phallus of the sun." [109]

[107] Saunders, Nicholas J. *Animal Spirits.* Boston: Little Brown & Company 1995, 62-63.
[108] Olcott, William Tyler. *Sun Lore of All Ages.* New York: G.P. Putnam's Sons 1914, 157
[109] Ibid., 294

The lion was also important to the early Britons during the Dark Ages and figures in the Merlin-Arthur chronicles. It should be noted, that as the lion was not a natural animal in the British Isles, its symbolism was imported from elsewhere.

Another lion-like beast, the griffin, is also represented among the various symbols in architectural motifs. Evans indicates that the griffin is associated with "carnal passion." In addition, according to Evans, griffins "are the demons that, in the form of winged lions, flew aloft on the pinions of pride and fell from heaven into the abyss of hell for their misdeeds." [110] Bullfinch wrote in *The Age of Fable* that the griffin originated in India and that they built their nests of gold. Bullfinch stated, "their instinct led them to know where buried treasures lay..." [111] However, Bullfinch did not equate the griffin with "carnal passion." Saunders notes that the griffin was also regarded by Medieval Christians as a symbol the "dual human/divine nature of Christ." [112]

The griffin was also representative of the elements of the earth and the air and, to the Graeco-Roman world, was associated with the sun god Apollo. Among other things, the griffin was regarded as a guardian by the Minoans and the Greeks and was associated as well with the goddess Athene.

Benton notes that griffins, while popular in medieval art, were not popular as gargoyles. [113] They did continue to be important images on heraldic devices, however but only occasionally served as gargoyles.

Griffin-demon images have been found in the royal palace of the Assyrian king Assurnasirpal dating from the 9th century BCE. These figures represent the Seven Sages of ancient Babylon.

---

[110] Evans, op cit., 39.
[111] Bullfinch, Thomas. *The Age of Fable.* New York: Nelson Doubleday 1968, 133.
[112] Saunders, Nicholas J. *Animal Spirits.* Boston: Little Brown & Company 1995, 150.
[113] Benton, Janetta Rebold. *Holy Terrors Gargoyles on Medieval Buildings.* New York: Abbeville Press 1997, 115.

A griffin carved on the Westminster Presbyterian façade 1300 N Street 1927.

The Seven Sages, according to Babylonian tradition, lived before the flood and appeared "from the sea in the 'first days.'" [114] In the Epic of Gilgamesh, the Seven Sages were said to have built the walls of the Babylonian city of Uruk.

---

[114] Black, Jeremy and Anthony Green. *Gods, Demons and Symbols of Ancient Mesopotamia.* University of Texas Press 1992, 163.

Man and griffin, ca. 1930, at the Sutter Club, 1220 9ᵀʰ Street.

The photo above, photographed at the Sutter Club, shows a kneeling man turning away from a griffin, reluctantly letting go of one of the griffin's wings. Evans would write of a similar sculpture found in the Freiburg Minster that "shows a man contending against a griffin, which signifies the effort to overcome carnal passion."[115]

Martin Henig suggests that griffins are symbolic agents of death.[116]

The winged lion is another ancient symbol that has been used in architectural art. While the early Christian church used the winged lion to represent the "Saviour's majesty", it was used much earlier by the Babylonians. Babylonian seals show the god Marduk riding upon a winged, fire belching lion, as well as Marduk fighting a

---

z

[115] Evans, op cit., 192.
[116] Henig, Martin. *Religion in Roman Britain.* New York; St. Martin's Press 1984, 105.

51

winged-lion. Evans remarks that "the colossal winged lions of Nineveh and Persepolis, originated in the priestly proclivity to symbolize and to express mystical ideas in material forms..." [117]

In Hebrew symbolism, the winged lion represents the Lion of Judah, or the Southerly direction. Christian lore adopted the winged lion also as the Lion of Judah representing St. Mark. Benton notes that while winged lions were occasionally crafted into gargoyles such as those on the Cathedral of Saint-Pierre in Poitiers, France, "there is no evidence that it was intended to represent Mark..." [118] because of its close proximity to other less religiously inspired figures. It was, perhaps, simply created because the stonemason desired to do so.

A winged lion carved on the Westminster Presbyterian church façade, 1300 N Street 1927.

---

[117] Evans, op cit., 10.
[118] Benton, Janetta Rebold. *Holy Terrors: Gargoyles on Medieval Buildings.* New York: Abbeville Press 1997, 119.

The Ram

The ram is well represented as a pagan symbol in western architecture. The ram is also one of the most recognized and disputed symbols is history. While Evans states that the ram symbolizes "spiritual leadership" [119] for early Christians, Barbara Walker, in *The Women's Encyclopedia of Myths and Secrets*, notes that the ram is "one of the 'horney' animals embodying the phallic god...."[120] She also states that the Egyptians referred to the ram as Amen-Ra, "the Ram, the virile male, the holy phallus, which stirreth up the passion of love, the Ram of rams." Before the Christian church turned these ancient symbols into caricatures of evil, the God of the Jews wore ram's horns and the Jewish armies were led into battle by priests using ram's horns "to make victory magic." [121]

In ancient Egyptian and other North African paintings and carvings, it is common to find the ram represented with the sun-disk placed between its horns. Campbell mentions that one of the sacred beasts of the Upper Nile was the ram. [122] Amon became associated with the ram after the god disguised himself as the animal and then announced to the world that the ram was sacred "except once a year, when a ram was flayed and beheaded in offering to him." [123] Saunders writes, "The ram was one of the first objects of cult worship, as is evident from 10,000-year-old Saharan rock paintings which depict humans worshipping a ram with a solar disk between its horns." [124]

---

[119] Evans, op cit, 76.

[120] Walker, Barbara G. *Encyclopedia of Women's Myths and Secrets.* New Jersey: Castle Books 1996, 841.

[121] Ibid.

[122] Campbell, Joseph. *The Masks of God: Primitive Mythology.* New York: Viking Press 1959, 382

[123] Veronica Ions, *Egyptian Mythology.* Middlesex: Paul Hamlyn, 1968, 94. See also Frazer, *The Golden Bough* pages 500-501 wherein he states that the images of Ammon appearing with the body of a man and the head of a ram "only shows that he was in the usual chrysalis state through which beast-gods regularly pass before they emerge as full-blown anthropomorphic gods. The ram, therefore, was killed, not as a sacrifice to Ammon, but as the god himself...."

[124] Saunders, op cit., 94.

The Ram was the symbol of the thunder god to the Yoruba of Africa. The ram is also associated with the Norse god Thor and the Egyptian god Khnum—both closely associated with thunder. [125] Khnum was self-created and created the heavens, the earth and the underworld...being as well the creator of all that is and all that will be. Being represented by a ram standing on its hind legs, Khnum was "the living soul of Ra."

Viaud notes that the ram was thought to contain the soul of Osiris. "Thoth himself, said his priests, had formerly decreed that the kings should come with offerings to the 'living ram'." [126] The ram was depicted in Egyptian art as representing Amon when the image was that of a ram with curved horns, and Khnum, Hershef or Haraphes when depicted with wavy horns.

The ram was also an important cult-animal of the Celts. John X.W.P. Corcoran wrote in his article *Celtic Mythology* "the ram enjoyed considerable importance as a cult animal among the Celts and was frequently associated with the horned god Cernunnos...Its connection with fertility rites are age old." [127]

The photo below shows an impressive ram decorating the Hotel Regis, a building constructed in 1912 at 1106 Eleventh Street, Sacramento. The Hotel Regis is listed on the National Register of Historic Places. The ram is adorned in royal splendor befitting the representative of both pagan and Christian deities.

In addition, the ram is associated with the Tibetan goddess Khon-ma, ruler over earth-demons, who, dressed in golden-yellow robes and carrying a giant noose, rode on a ram. The ram is symbolic of renewing fertility and the returning warmth of the sun and is associated with the ancient gods Baal and Ea in the Middle East, Indra and Agni in India and Apollo in Greece. The ram was sacred to Zeus, Pan and Dionysus—all known for their powers of

[125] Biedermann, Hans. *Dictionary of Symbolism: Cultural Icons & The Meanings Behind Them.* New York: Meridian 1994, 278
[126] Viaud, J. "Egyptian Mythology: The Sacred Animals", in *New Larousse Encyclopedia of Mythology.* London: Prometheus Press 1959, 45.
[127] Corcoran, John X.W.P. "Celtic Mythology", in *New Larousse Encyclopedia of Mythology.* London: Prometheus Press 1959, 239

fertility. The ram was also a sacrificial animal in Islam and in the Old Testament where it became a substitute for Isaac.

In Christianity, it was a symbol of Jesus as leader of the flock.[128]

A ram appears as a gargoyle at the Church of Saint-Ouen in Rouen, France where the figure has a human face—another of the composite creatures created with an unknown meaning.

Hotel Regis ram, 1106 Eleventh Street (1912).

---

[128] Cooper, J.C. *An Illustrated Encyclopaedia of Traditional Symbols.* London: Thames and Hudson 1978, 136.

Another interesting figure (shown above) adorning the front of Masonic Temple at 1123 J Street in Sacramento constructed in 1920 depicts a small child resting between the horns of a ram. This appears to have been a Christianization of an ancient Egyptian symbol. The sun-disk was often displayed between the ram's horns but in this image a child, or "son," sits between the curved horns. There is a duality of meaning in these depictions of the ram being both symbolic of Jesus leading the flock and in other Christian lore identifying the ram with "lustful sinners" and the devil.

The Bear

Another symbolic animal, the bear, is found in abundance throughout California. This is not unusual, as the Golden Bear is prominently displayed on the state flag and is well known as the California state symbol. However, the bear as an important icon is almost a universal figure around the world.

Evans noted that the bear, at least in Christian mythology, is synonymous with the devil. Evans describes one relief on the door of a cathedral in Hildesheim, carved in 1015, which depicts "a bear stand(ing) behind Pilate, whispering into his ear and filing his mind with diabolical suggestions." [129]

However, according to Geoffrey Ashe in his book *Dawn Behind The Dawn,* the she bear is identified as "an ancient maternal symbol" [130] and the bear in general is one of the oldest identified deities. This is evident in the pre-historic altars found in cave settings that have bear skulls arranged carefully around and on top of the altars. The importance of the bear is deeply rooted in ancient cultures from Japan to Siberia and eastward to include Native Americans.

The bear is a symbol of creation, rebirth, wisdom and fertility among ancient cultures. The bear is also associated with the goddess Artemis and because of this, was sacred to the Greeks.

Among the Norse, the "berserkers" went into battle "dressed only in bear skins, yet...remains unharmed by sword or fire." Christians in the Dark Ages believed that the bear was, according to Saunders, "a cruel and vicious animal, an image of carnality and the devil." [131] However, the bear was also of symbolic importance in the legends of the Christian saints Gall, Columban, Ursinus, Sergius, Corbinian, Hubertus and Maximin of Trier.

Campbell records that the Athapaskan people of British Columbia believed that the bear was the guardian of fire. [132] The bear was also regarded as a spirit guide by the Native Americans, and like the ram, is representative of the Celtic deities of war, revenge and smithing.

Our bear figure on page 59 is shown on the front of the Capitol National Bank, designed by Rudolph Herold who also designed the Masonic Temple and City Hall, appears to represent an ancient maternal symbol. Looking very benign, the bear is shown with two children climbing onto its back, apparently for a ride. Interesting as well are the spiral patterns, which surround the bear and children.

---

[129] Evans, op cit., 88
[130] Ashe, Geoffrey. *Dawn Behind the Dawn: A Search for the Earthly Paradise.* New York; Henry Holt and Company, Inc. 1992, 30
[131] Saunders, op cit. 76.
[132] Campbell, op cit. 338.

The spiral as it appears in this carving represents the "web of life and the veil of the Mother Goddess, controller of destiny and weaver of the veil of illusion." [133] The photo reflects the Bear Mother, which is not only present in most Native American mythology but also in Old Norse stories. Christopher Manes wrote in *Other Creations: Rediscovering the Spirituality of Animals*, that the Bear Mother is representative of the Mother Goddess. [134]

Manes continues:

"Invariably, the feminine animal spirit represents a force for good, even cultural heroism. In the Bear Mother stories....a woman is kidnapped by a bear in the form of a man, who takes her to his village to be his bride. In her new life among the bears, the woman learns their 'songs,' at the same time teaching the bear spirits about human society. The woman usually gives birth to several children by her bear husband who grow up to become leaders or warriors." [135]

The bear is perhaps the most ancient of the sacred animals. Cave paintings dating to 32,000-75,000 BP in France and discovery of the intentional arrangement of bear skulls on rock altars, also in caves, indicates that the bear cult was active at least 32 millennium ago in Europe. The bear cult has continued as an important part of the indigenous Ainu culture in Japan. The Ainu, direct decendents of the ancient Jomōn culture, are possibly related to the Tlingit Indians of Alaska who are well known for their artistic renderings of the bear in their tribal art. The bear in Ainu belief is the god of the mountain, a sacred messenger and culture hero. During one of the Ainu ceremonies, called the *iyomante,* a bear is ritually slain so that its soul is sent back to the land of the gods. There are many legends among indigenous people around the world that tell of a human woman mating with a bear and producing offspring. The Ainu have a similar story. Sir James Frazer wrote, "they have a legend of a woman who had a son by a bear; and many of them who dwell in the mountains pride themselves on being descended from a bear. Such

[133] Cooper, op cit., 156.
[134] Manes, Christopher. *Other Creations: Rediscovering the Spirituality of Animals.* New York: Doubleday 1997, 162-163.
[135] Ibid.

people are called "Descendents of the bear"…, and in the pride of their heart they will say, "As for me, I am a child of the god of the mountains…" [136]

Children playing on the back of the Bear Mother, Capitol National Bank, 700 J Street, 1915.

The bear as a sacrificial animal is not only important to the Ainu but to the Delaware Indians living in Ontario, Canada. During the Big House ceremony, which is held at Hagersville, Ontario on the first full moon in January, a hibernating bear is driven from its den, brought to the Big House and killed with a blow to the head. It bear is eaten in a ceremonial meal and its spirit "rises to Patamawas ('to whom prayers are offered'), bearing with it the prayers of mankind."[137]

---

[136] Frazer, Sir James. *The Golden Bough: A study in magic and religion.* Hertfordshire: Wordsworth Editions 1993, 505-506.
[137] Krickberg, Walter & et al. *Pre-Columbian American Religions.* New York: Holt, Rinehart and Winston 1968, 166.

The bear is viewed as a lunar power around the world and the astronomical signs of the Big House ceremony indicate this is true to North American Indians as well.

The bear is associated with resurrection (due to its hibernating ability), and thus with rebirth and renewal. It also is known for its supernatural powers, strength, bravery and stamina. It was sacred to Artemis and Diana—both goddesses of nature. Young Greek girls used to dance to Artemis in the guise of bears, wearing both bear masks and bear costumes and were called "Arktoi", meaning "she-bears." [138] Norse warriors also dressed in bearskins for battle and were so fierce and impervious to sword and fire that they became known as "berserkers."

In Mongolian shamanism, the bear is regarded as lord of the animals and is revered as an ancestor. The bear is called *baabgai,* which means "father." Stewart tells us that the Mongolians regard the literal name for the bear as taboo, "given that the bear is recognized as an ancestor by almost all Siberian peoples." [139] While the bear is hunted at times it is also treated with great respect, the skulls placed on poles or in trees or placed on a platform as shamans are after death. Like the dog in some cultures, the bear is believed by some Siberian people to oversee the journey of the soul to the underworld.

The bear is a messenger of forest spirits in shamanism and this concept carried over to the Slavic traditions. The *Leshii,* that fairy-like shape-changer who was master of the forest and protector of animals, used both the wolf and the bear as special servants. The bear would not only serve the Leshii but also protect him.

Inuit and Lapp shamans will shape-shift into bear form for their spirit journeys.

Like the Mongolians, the use of the "regular" name for the bear in Apache culture was also prohibited. According to ethnologist Morris Edward Opler, "...the Chiricahua would seldom say the

---

[138] Baring, Anne and Jules Cashford. *The Myth of the Goddess: Evolution of an Image.* London: Arkana/Penguin Books 1991, 326.

[139] Sarangerel (Julie Ann Stewart). *Riding Windhorses: A Journey into the Heart of Mongolian Shamanism.* Rochester: Destiny Books 2000, 33.

regular word for bear. They would call it 'mother's sibling.' It doesn't like to be called by the regular word. It gets after you when you say that." [140] In other words, the bear will cause illness if it is addressed directly with its regular name. The Apache did not hunt, eat or use the skins of bear and avoided it as much as possible. According to one of Opler's informants, "If you come in contact with the track of a bear, or a tree where the bear has leaned, or bear manure, or if you sleep where a bear has sat down, or if you come in contact with a bear by smell or touch, you can get sick." [141]

Like many other sacred icons of other more ancient religions, the bear, in Christian theology, represented the Devil, evil, cruelty and carnal appetite. Evans describes one relief on the door of a cathedral in Hildesheim, carved in 1015, "which depicts a bear stand(ing) behind Pilate, whispering into his ear and filing his mind with diabolical suggestions." [142]

While it may seem incongruous that the bear, known for its size and savagery, has been worshipped for its Mother Goddess aspects it is the loving relationship that the adult bear has with its young that denotes this special association. Tamra Andrews noted "Bears were almost always connected in some way to the female life force, either being female themselves and giving birth or being the offspring of a human female. This quality reinforced the bears' intimate connection with fertility, renewal, and, often, the moon." [143]

The goddess Artio ("bear goddess"), worshipped in the Berne (Celtic for "bear") area of Switzerland during the 4th century CE, was the protectress of bears against hunters. She also protected humans from the wrath of the bear! Artio was a goddess of plenty, which ties into the bear's associations with fertility and renewal. Bear amulets have been found in North Britain and other areas and

---

[140] Opler, Morris Edward. *An Apache Life-Way: The Economic, Social, and Religious Institutions of the Chiricahua Indians.* Chicago: The University of Chicago Press 1941, 224.

[141] Ibid. 225.

[142] Evans, E.P. *Animal Symbolism in Ecclesiastical Architecture.* London: W. Heineman 1896, 88.

[143] Andrews, Tamra. *A Dictionary of Nature Myths.* Oxford: Oxford University Press 1998, 25.

have been found in burials. A small child was found buried near Malton in Yorkshire with a tiny black bear-amulet [144] showing perhaps the belief that the bear helped the soul on its way to the underworld.

Aside from the Apache, the bear was an important spiritual totem to many Native American people. The bear is associated with sacred and powerful water sites and was regarded as a major deity and source of power. Bear doctors could shape-shift from human to bear by swimming in a special pool. Once in the water the doctor would emerge in a bear form and could only change back into his human form by submerging once again in the same pool. The bear has many of the characteristics of water. It is symbolic of rebirth and renewal; it is connected to the feminine life force and fertility. The bear was thought to be the creator of geysers in California; the spirit of the bear was believed to heat the water for curative purposes, which were utilized extensively by the local tribes.

In Lakota belief, the bear "is the friend of the Great Spirit. He is very wise." [145] The bear instructed the shaman in ceremonial secrets, song and medicines. To the Lakota, if a man sees a bear in his dreams or visions he must become a medicine man. The Lakota believe that the bear is the only creature that knows all things about the Great Spirit and is totally conversant in the language of the shaman. The bear is referred to as "the God the Bear," and presides over "love and hate and bravery and wounds and many kinds of medicines." He was also "the patron of mischief and fun." [146]

"The Bears" is one of the Oglala Sioux sodalities, a "dream cult" made up of individuals who have had the same vision. Called the *Mato ihanblapi* ("they dream of bears") the members would dress for their ceremonies as bears, parade around the camp, growling like bears while they chased people. According to Powers, these "bear dreamers" were "astute curers." [147]

---

[144] Green, Miranda. *The Gods of the Celts.* Glouchester: Alan Sutton 1986, 184.
[145] Walker, James R. *Lakota Belief and Ritual.* Lincoln: University of Nebraska Press 1991, 116.
[146] Ibid, 121.
[147] Powers, William K. *Oglala Religion.* Lincoln: University of Nebraska Press 1982, 58.

At one California Miwok site located just Northeast of Sacramento, a large standing stone called the "Northstar stone" was used for ceremonial purposes. It stands with several mortars (areas used for the grinding of food and other materials) on one side, two on the top, and with several incised lines that run the length of one side. It is believed that this stone was a central piece used during bear ceremonies thanking the Grizzly Bear and to welcome the change of season from winter to spring. The mortars were used to grind berries and other food items with the juices running down the incised lines into a catchment at the bottom. It is assumed that the Grizzly was lured into the area and would eat from the catchment, performing its part in the ritual. A bear "footprint" (photo below) was carved into one portion of the Northstar stone representative of a bear walking in a docile manner, the back print overlapping with the print of the forepaw.

The footprint and incised grooves on Northstar are similar to other "rain rocks" found in Northern California. A similar bear footprint carving is located in Northwestern California and a large carving representing the claw marks of a bear can be seen at Chaw'se, Indian Grinding Rock State Park near Fiddletown, California.

The importance of the bear in Native American culture and religion cannot be minimized. During an archaeological excavation in 1966 in the Sacramento delta area east of Oakley, California, a Plains Miwok burial of a small, five-year old Indian girl was uncovered. The unusual aspect of this burial was that the child was buried with a Grizzly Bear cub of approximately the same size. It appeared to the excavators that the bear cub was slain deliberately to accompany the child to the afterlife. According to the excavation report, the bear was positioned directly behind and to the side of the child with one paw draped over the child's body. [148] To the Plains Indians the bear is believed to be the ruler of underworld creatures so its association with death and the underworld may have been instrumental for its inclusion in the child's burial.

The Athapaskan Indians of British Columbia believe the bear to be the guardian of fire; however, it is the "Bear Mother" that remains the most endearing characterization of this animal. Christopher Manes wrote that the Bear Mother is representative of the Mother Goddess. According to Manes:

---

[148] Cowan, R.A., Clewlow, C.W. Jr. & et al. "An Unusual Burial of a Bear and Child From the Sacramento Delta", in Institute of Archaeology, University of California Los Angeles Journal of New World Archaeology, Vol 1, Number 2, December 1975, 25-30.

"Invariably, the feminine animal spirit represents a force for good, even cultural heroism. In the Bear Mother stories....a woman is kidnapped by a bear in the form of a man, who takes her to his village to be his bride. In her new life among the bears, the woman learns their 'songs,' at the same time teaching the bear spirits about human society. The woman usually gives birth to several children by her bear husband who grow up to become leaders or warriors."[149]

The Dragon

We have previously discussed the dragon but the dragon as an icon deserves some special attention here as well. While dragons are commonly associated with the Orient, and rightfully so, it is in London where the dragon is so commonly seen carved on building facades, steeples and city gates.

"The dragon," wrote Janetta Benton, "was depicted more requently in medieval art than any other fantastic creature." [150] What is the origin for the dragon in medieval legend and folklore? Why did the dragon assume such an important place in humankind's vast repertoire of fantastic beasts and monsters? The dragon has been called the primal enemy of man, "an opponent of human heroes." [151] The dragon, in legend, is at once a supernatural creature born of the earth and a real creature of the animal kingdom fighting for its survival in a world increasingly pushing into its domain.

In ancient Greek myth, the dragon guards the Golden Fleece and this treasure guarding aspect is commonly repeated in Old English and Norse sagas through the Middle Ages. In Christian lore the dragon, even though seen as symbolic of evil, was a guardian of knowledge. [152] In a previous age it was believed that legends concerning dragon were a "race memory" of a time when man lived

---

[149] Manes, op cit., 162-163.

[150] Benton, Janetta Rebold. *Holy Terrors: Gargoyles on Medieval Buildings*. New York: Abbeville Press 1997, 103.

[151] Evans, Jonathan. "Dragon" in *Medieval Folklore: A Guide to Myths, Legends, Tales, Beliefs, and Customs*. Oxford: Oxford University Press 2000, 100.

[152] Gibson, Clare. *The Hidden Life of Art: Secrets and Symbols in Great Masterpieces*. New York: Barnes & Noble Books/Saraband (Scotland) Ltd. 2006, 142.

alongside the dinosaur until it was determined that millions of years separated the two. However, there may be some truth to this theory if we consider that fossils of dinosaurs have been uncovered for thousands of years and would have demanded some explanation. How else to explain the remains of a T-Rex, an allosaur or a raptor?

Do the many depictions of dragons as grotesques and gargoyles in Britain and throughout Europe indicate that people of the Middle Ages believed in their existence? Benton notes, "Medieval reports of fabulous creatures were as detailed and descriptive as those of actual animals. In art, the dragon that Saint George slays is shown to be as believable as the horse on which he rides." [153]

However, she continues, "gargoyle imagery, like other imagery in medieval art, had little to do with direct observation of the natural world," but, rather "emphasis was, above all, on the moral edification a creature provided." [154]

The answer to our question as to the origin of the dragon in medieval legend may be simple misidentification. In an article in the January 18, 1851 edition of the British periodical *Notes and Queries* a contributor wrote:

"...mention is made, in the account of the church of St. Maria delle Grazie, near Mantua, of a stuffed lizard, crocodile, or other reptile, which is preserved suspended in the church. This is said to have been killed in the adjacent swamps, about the year 1406. It is stated to be six or seven feet long.

"At the west door of the cathedral of Cracow are hanging some bones, said to have belonged to the dragon which inhabited the cave at the foot of the rock (the Wawel) on which the cathedral and the royal castle stand; and was destroyed by Krak, the founder of the city.

"It has struck me as possible that the real history of these crocodiles or alligators, if they are such, may be, that they were brought home by crusaders as specimens of dragons, just as Henry the Lion, Duke of Brunswick, brought from the Holy Land the antelope's horn which had been palmed upon him as a specimen of a

---

[153] Benton, op cit 122-125.
[154] Ibid., 125

griffin's claw, and which may still be seen in the cathedral of that city. That they should afterwards be fitted with appropriate legends, is not surprising." [155]

Another contributor to the same journal noted "…the head of a dragon said to have been strangled by St. Martha's garter, and preserved with great veneration at Alix, is undoubtedly the fossilized head of an extinct Saurian reptile." [156] In addition, the writer mentioned that several "continental churches" with reputations of containing the preserved bodies of dragons, "shown as dragons killed by saints" were, in reality, parts of preserved crocodiles. Undoubtedly, any crocodile encountered by a knight during the Crusades would have been an adversary to be reckoned with.

While the actual artifacts of supposed dragon remains may be the bodies of unfortunate crocodiles, the legends are based on much older traditions dating back thousands of years before the Crusades—traditions firmly entrenched in the human mind and expressed in the form of gargoyles and grotesques.

Ancient mythology and folklore concerned with dragons can be traced back to the days of ancient Babylon. Historian Fred Gladstone Skinner tells us that the Hittite dragon was associated with rivers and was celebrated seasonally in a festival called Puruli. He wrote, "the ritual of the slaying of the dragon, if enacted each year, would guarantee that the rivers would stay within their bounds."[157]

Legends of dragons slain by a cultural hero (including Saints) became universal over time. "In many communities of modern Europe," he continues, "the slaying of the dragon is enacted in an annual pageant…" A primeval "Dragon goddess", known as Tiâmat, was worshipped in ancient Babylon…in what is now devastated Iraq. As evil as Satan, she was described as a "she-devil…revolting in appearance, and evil in every way." [158] However,

---

[155] "Dragons" in *Notes and Queries,* vol. 3 (64) Jan 18 1851, page 40.
[156] "Is it a Fossil?" in *Notes and Queries,* vol.73rd (165) Feb 25 1865, page 158.
[157] Skinner, Fred Gladstone. *Myths and Legends of the Ancient Near East.* New York: Barnes & Noble Books 1993, 158, 159.

while she was the "personification of chaos, night, darkness and inertness" [159] Tiâmat was also the "Universe-Mother." The Dragon goddess was linked to the dead and had in her possession the Tablet of Fate on which the fate of even man was written before the creation of the world. Similar characteristics have been associated with Europe's dragons as well. In Germanic lore, the fiery dragon was regarded as the guardian of the burial mound. [160] It was this dragon with fiery breath, pointed tail and folded wings that Beowulf killed before he, himself, died—the same image that has played such an important part in our contemporary literature and fairy tale.

A Sacramento dragon grotesque, ca. 1914. Located at the El Cortez Apartments this dragon keeps company with many Green Men on its façade and is near the Sacramento cathedral.

[158] Budge, E. A. Wallis. *Babylonian Life and History.* New York: Barnes & Noble Books 2005, 63.
[159] Ibid.
[160] Davidson, H. R. Ellis. *Gods and Myths of the Viking Age.* New York: Bell Publishing Company 1981, 159.

Because of these ancient legends, the dragon became an important icon for thousands of years. It still finds itself carved upon our buildings as grotesque and gargoyle and in our psyche.

Like many ancient symbols, the dragon in Christian theology represents "the issue of evil, the essence of the devil and mankind's enemy, the dragon does not exist in the natural world, but remains a metaphor for evil in its many forms." [161]

The Westminster Presbyterian Church on N Street is perhaps the most densely populated building in terms of iconography in Sacramento. Several images of religious meaning festoon the front and roof of the church. The photographs on the next few pages show just a few of the ancient Christian symbols that can be found at this location.

---

[161] O'Connell, Mark and Raje Airey. *The Complete Encyclopedia of Signs & Symbols.* London: Hermes House 2005, 140.

70

AFTERWORD

Cities offer much more than traffic, bedroom communities and employment opportunities. Cities such as Sacramento also offer a world of wonder—if we look for it. The Green Men, grotesques and other architectural wonders dating back one hundred fifty years and more provide a look not only at our immediate past, but the past experienced in by-gone ages.

These works were limited only by the artisan's imagination and skill. They are profound links to other times and other cultures and to the dreams and beliefs of those who made them as well as to those who continue to appreciate the vast assortment of images left on the buildings we use to this day.

Please take some time and look around—you may be surprised at what you see and how much there is. Let us strive to protect these works for future visitors and residents of Sacramento.

APPENDIX
FIGURE LOCATIONS

ADDRESS	PHOTO *PAGE*
Old Town, 1015-17 Front Street	20, 45
801 I Street	
828 I Street	32
631 J Street	48
700 J Street	59
1123 J Street	33, 56
1230 J Street [162]	
717 K Street	31
1301 L Street	
800 N Street	
1100 N Street	
1300 N Street	50, 52, 69, 70, 71
1006 4th Street	

---

[162] When an address is listed with no page number an image can be found at that address but no corresponding photograph is in this guide.

923 7th Street   17

1220 9th Street   38, 51

921 11th Street

1100 11th Street   29, 30, 68

1106 11th Street   55

BIBLIOGRAPHY

Addy, S.O. "A Yorkshire Village", in *The Gentleman's Magazine*, Vol. CCLXVII, July to December. London: Chatto & Windus, Piccadilly 1889, 34

Alexander, Marc. *A Companion to the Folklore, Myths & Customs of Britain.* Phoenix Mill: Sutton Publishing Limited 2002

Anderson, M.D. *History and Imagery in British Churches.* London: John Murray Ltd.1971

Anderson, William. *Green Man: The Archetype of our oneness with the Earth.* London and San Francisco: Harper Collins 1990

Andrews, Tamra. *A Dictionary of Nature Myths.* Oxford: Oxford University Press 1998,

Ashe, Geoffrey. *Dawn Behind The Dawn: A Search for the Earthly Paradise.* New York: Henry Holt and Company, Inc. 1992

Ballard, Carol. *The Geen Man: The Shakespeare Connection.* Warwickshire: Self published 1999

Baring-Gould, S. *Curious Myths of the Middle Ages.* New York: John B. Alden, Publishers 1885

Basford, Kathleen H. "Quest For The Green Man", in *Symbols of Power.* H.R. Ellis Davidson, editor. Cambridge: D.S. Brown Ltd.1977 pp 101-120

Basford, Kathleen. *The Green Man.* Cambridge: D.S. Brewer 1978

Beck, Horace. *Folklore and the Sea.* Mystic: Mystic Seaport Museum Incorporated 1973

Benton, Janetta Rebold. *Holy Terrors: Gargoyles on Medieval Buildings.* New York: Abbeville Press 1997

Benton, Janetta Rebold. *Art of the Middle Ages.* London: Thames & Hudson Ltd. 2002

Bernard, Penny. "Mermaids, Snakes and the Spirits of the Water in Southern Africa: Implications for River Health", lecture given in *Shortcourse on the Role and Use of Aquatic Biomonitoring.* Rhodes University, Grahamstown, South Africa 2000

Biedermann, Hans. *Dictionary of Symbolism: Cultural Icons & The Meanings Behind Them.* New York: Meridian 1994

Bienville, Michael de. *Gargoyles.* Kansas City: Andrews and McMeel 1996

Black, Jeremy &Anthony Green. *Gods, Demons and Symbols of Ancient Mesopotamia.* Austin: University of Texas Press 1992

Blackwood, John. *Oxford's Gargoyles and Grotesques.* Oxford: Charon Press 1986

Bord, Janet and Colin. *Earth Rites: Fertility Practices in Pre-Industrial Britain.* London: Granada Publishing Limited 1982

Brewster, Harry. *The River Gods of Greece: Myths and Mountain Waters in the Hellenic World.* London: I.B. Tauris & Co. Ltd. 1997

Bridaham, Lester Burbank. *Gargoyles, Chimeres, and the Grotesque in French Gothic Sculpture.* New York: Architectural Book Publishing Company, Inc. 1930

Budge, E. A. Wallis. *Babylonian Life and History.* New York: Barnes & Noble Books 2005

Bullfinch, Thomas. *The Age of Fable.* New York: Nelson Doubleday 1968

Campbell, Joseph. *The Hero With a Thousand Faces.* New York: MJF Books 1949

Campbell, Joseph. *The Masks of God: Creative Mythology.* London: Secker & Warburg, 1968

Campbell, Joseph *The Masks of God: Primitive Mythology.* New York: Viking Press, 1959

Campbell, Joseph *The Masks of God: Occidental Mythology.* New York: Viking Press, 1964

Campbell, Joseph *The Masks of God: Oriental Mythology.* New York: Viking Press, 1962

Carrington, Richard. *Mermaids and Mastodons: A Book of Natural & Unnatural History.* New York: Rinehart & Company, Inc. 1957

Carrington , Richard "The Natural History of the Mermaid", in Horizon, January, 1960, Vol. II, Number 3, 131

Cave, C.J.P. *Medieval Carvings in Exeter Cathedral.* London: Penguin Books 1953

Champneys, Arthur C. *Irish Ecclesiastical Architecture.* New York: Hacker Art Books/Irish University Press 1970

Conway, D.J. *Celtic Magic.* St. Paul: Llewellyn Publications, 1990

Conway, D.J *Maiden, Mother, Crone: The Myth & Reality of the Triple Goddess.* St. Paul: Llewellyn Publications 1995

Cooper, J.C. *An Illustrated Encyclopaedia of Traditional Symbols.* New York: Thames and Hudson 1978

Corcoran, John X.W.P. "Celtic Mythology", in *New Larousse Encyclopedia of Mythology.* London: Prometheus Press 1959 pp 222-244

Coughlan, Robert. *The World of Michelangelo 1475-1564.* New York: Time-Life Books 1966

Cowan, R.A., Clewlow, C.W. Jr. & et al. "An Unusual Burial of a Bear and Child From the Sacramento Delta", in Institute of Archaeology, University of California Los Angeles Journal of New World Archaeology, Vol 1, Number 2, December 1975, 25-30.

Crowley, Vivianne. *Phoenix From the Flame: Pagan Spirituality in the Western World.* London/San Francisco: The Aquarian Press/Harper Collins Publishers 1994

Cunliffe, Barry. *The Ancient Celts.* New York: Oxford University Press, 1997

Cunningham, Scott. *Cunningham's Encyclopedia of Magical Herbs.* St. Paul: Llewellyn Publications 1985

Davidson, H. R. Ellis. *Gods and Myths of the Viking Age.* New York: Bell Publishing Company 1981

Doel, Fran & Geoff. *The Green Man in Britain.* Gloucestershire: Tempus Publishing Ltd. 2001

Eisler, Riane. *The Chalice and the Blade: Our History, Our Future.* San Francisco: Harper Collins 1987

Ellerbe, Helen. *The Dark Side of Christian History.* Orlando: Morningstar and Lark 1995

Evans, E.P. *Animal Symbolism in Ecclesiastical Architecture.* London: W. Heineman 1896

Evans, Jonathan. "Dragon" in *Medieval Folklore: A Guide to Myths, Legends, Tales, Beliefs, and Customs.* Oxford: Oxford University Press 2000

Fiske, John. *Myths and Myth-Makers: Old Tales and Superstitions Interpreted by Comparative Mythology.* Boston: Houghton, Mifflin and Company 1881

Floyd, E. Randall. *Great Southern Mysteries.* Little Rock: August House Publishers 1989

Frazer, Sir James. *The Golden Bough: A Study in Magic and Religion.* Hertfordshire: Wordsworth Reference, Wordsworth Editions Ltd. 1993

Gibson, Clare. *The Hidden Life of Art: Secrets and Symbols in Great Masterpieces.* New York: Barnes & Noble Books/Saraband (Scotland) Ltd. 2006

Giorgi, Rosa. *Angels and Demons in Art.* Los Angeles: The J. Paul Getty Museum 2005

Goodyear, W.H. *Roman and Medieval Art.* Meadville: The Chautaugua-Century Press 1893

Graves, Robert,ed. *New Larousse Encyclopedia of Mythology.* London: Prometheus Press 1959

Green, Miranda. *The Gods of the Celts.* Glouchester: Alan Sutton 1986

Grundy, Thirlie. *Going in Search of the Green Man in Cumbria.* Cumbria: Thumbprint 2000

Grundy, Thirlie. *The Green Man in Northumberland and County Durham.* Carlisle Cumbria: Thumbprint 2001

Harte, Jeremy. *The Green Man.* Andover: Pitkin Unichrome Ltd 2001

Hicks, Clive. *The Green Man: A Field Guide.* Helhoughton: COMPASSbooks 2000

Henig, Martin. *Religion in Roman Britain.* New York: St. Martin's Press 1984

Hunt, Marjorie. *The Stone Carvers: Master Craftsmen of Washington National Cathedral.* Washington: Smithsonian Institution Press 1999

Husain, Shahrukh. *The Goddess.* Alexandria: Time-Life Books 1997

Hutton, Ronald. *The Pagan Religions of the Ancient British Isles: Their Nature and Legacy.* Oxford: Blackwell Publishers Ltd 1991

Ions, Veronica. *Egyptian Mythology.* Middlesex: Paul Hamlyn, 1968

Jaffe', Aniela. "Symbolism In The Visual Arts", in *Man and His Symbols,* Carl G. Jung, editor. New York: Doubleday & Company, 1964 pp 230-271

Jones, Malcolm. "Green Man" in *Medieval Folklore.* Oxford: Oxford University Press 2002

Jung, Carl G., ed. *Man and His Symbols.* New York: Doubleday & Company, 1964

Lintrop, Aado. "On the Udmurt Water Spirit and the Formation of the Concept 'Holy" Among Permian Peoples" in Folklore, Vol. 26, April 2004, 9. Published by the Folk Belief & Media Group of the Estonian Literary Museum, Tartu

MacDermott, Mercia. *Explore Green Men*. Loughborough: Explore Books/Heart of Albion Press 2003

Mackenzie, Donald A. *Crete & Pre-Hellenic Myths and Legends*. London: Senate/Random House 1995. Reprint of the 1917 edition published as *Crete & Pre-Hellenic Europe,* by The Gresham Publishing Company, London

Manes, Christopher. *Other Creations: Rediscovering the Spirituality of Animals.* New York: Doubleday 1997

Mann, Nicholas R. *His Story: Masculinity in the Post-Patriarchal World.* St. Paul: Llewellyn Publications 1995

Merriam, C. Hart. Editor. *The Dawn of the World: Myths and Tales of the Miwok Indians of California*. Lincoln: University of Nebraska Press 1993, pg. 228-230.

Messenger, John C. *Inis Beag: Isle of Ireland.* Case Studies in Cultural Anthropology. New York: Holt, Rinehart and Winston 1969

Mohen, Jean-Pierre. *The World of Megaliths.* New York: Facts on File, 1989

Murray-Aynsley, Mrs. *Symbolism of the East and West.* London: George Redway 1900

Newbury, P.E. *Appendix 2: Report on the floral wreaths found in the coffins of Tutankhamen,* in Howard Carter, *The Tomb of Tutankhamen,* Excalibur Books, 1972

O'Connell, Mark and Raje Airey. *The Complete Encyclopedia of Signs & Symbols.* London: Hermes House 2005

Olcott, William Tyler. *Sun Lore of All Ages: A Collection of Myths and Legends Concerning the Sun and Its Worship.* New York: G.P. Putnam's Sons 1914

Opler, Morris Edward. *An Apache Life-Way: The Economic, Social, and Religious Institutions of the Chiricahua Indians.* Chicago: The University of Chicago Press 1941

Osoba, Funmi. *Benin Folklore: A Collection of Classic Folktales and Legends.* London: Hadada Books 1993

Piccinini, Chiara. "Gargoyles" in *Medieval Folklore: A Guide to Myths, Legends, Tales, Beliefs, and Customs.* Oxford: Oxford University Press 2002

Rappoport, Angelo. *The Sea: Myths and Legends.* London: Senate 1995, 184. A reprint of the 1928 edition published by Stanley Paul & Company, London. Originally titled *Superstitions of Sailors*

Riccardo and Giulia Marrucchi. *Art of the Middle Ages.* Firenze: SCALA Group, S.p.A. 2007

Roosevelt, Theodore. *History as Literature and Other Essays.* New York; Charles Scribner's Sons 1913

Ruether, Rosemary Radford. *Gaia and God.* San Francisco: Harper Collins 1994

Sarangerel (Julie Ann Stewart). *Riding Windhorses: A Journey into the Heart of Mongolian Shamanism.* Rochester: Destiny Books 2000

Saunders. Nicholas J. *Animal Spirits.* Boston: Little Brown and Company 1995

Seznec, Jean. *The Survival of the Pagan Gods: The Mythological Tradition and Its Place in Renaissance Humanism and Art.* New York: Harper Torchbooks/The Bollingen Library 1961

Skinner, Fred Gladstone. *Myths and Legends of the Ancient Near East.* New York: Barnes & Noble Books 1993

Timpson, John. *Timpson's Leylines: A Layman Tracking the Ley's.* London: Cassell & Co. 2000

Varner, Gary R. *Sacred Wells: A Study in the History, Meaning, and Mythology of Holy Wells & Waters.* Baltimore: Publish America 2002

Viaud, J. "Egyptian Mythology: The Sacred Animals", in *New Larousse Encyclopedia of Mythology.* London: Prometheus Press 1959 pp 43-48

Walker, Barbara G. *The Women's Encyclopedia of Myths and Secrets,* New Jersey: Castle Books 1996

Walker, James R. *Lakota Belief and Ritual.* Lincoln: University of Nebraska Press 1991

Weir, Anthony and James Jerman. *Images of Lust: Sexual Carvings on Medieval Churches.* London: Routledge 1999

Yenne, Bill. *Gothic Gargoyles.* New York: Barnes & Noble Books 2000

INDEX

A

Africa, 37, 38, 41, 46, 53, 54
Apache, 60, 61, 62
Archetype, 5
architectural motif, 10, 20, 23, 46, 49
architectural styles, 7, 32
artisans, 6, 7, 28

B

Babylon, 34, 35, 49, 50, 51, 67
bear, 27, 56, 57, 58, 59, 60
Benin, 37
Black Death, 23
Botticelli, 26, 27, 28

C

California, 6, 17, 20, 28, 29, 38, 39, 40, 56, 62, 63, 64
Capital National Bank, 32
carvers, 9, 10, 11, 13, 14, 15, 16, 23, 24
cathedrals, 8, 12, 13, 16, 19, 20, 22, 23
cemeteries, 4
Cernunnos, 54
children, 18, 28, 40, 57, 58, 59, 64
Christian, 4, 11, 12, 13, 14, 18, 19, 20, 21, 22, 24, 25, 26, 27, 28, 29, 39, 43, 44, 46, 47, 49,
51, 52, 53, 54, 55, 56, 57, 61, 65, 68, 69
Christian symbolism, 4
City Hall, 31, 32, 57
Classical Revival, 47
composite creatures, 55
crocodile, 66, 67

D

demons, 8, 49, 54
devil, 8, 17, 18, 56, 57, 61, 67, 68
Dionysus, 54
dragon, 5, 8, 18, 19, 28, 64, 65, 66, 67, 68

E

ecclesiastical buildings, 5, 13, 28
ecclesiastical structures, 10, 14, 19
Egypt, 8, 47, 48, 53, 54, 56
El Cortez Apartments, 29, 68
England, 5, 17

F

figure locations, 72
foliate head, 20, 21, 23, 24, 25, 26, 28
folklore, 5, 6, 11, 34, 36, 37, 39, 65, 67
France, 8, 11, 26, 35, 43, 52, 55, 58

G

gargoyles, 5, 8, 9, 10, 11, 12, 13, 14, 15, 16, 17, 18, 20, 23, 49, 52, 65, 67
geysers, 62
Goddess, 36, 37, 42-44, 47, 48, 54, 57, 60, 61, 67
Gothic, 5, 8, 9, 12, 13, 16, 22, 26
Gothic Revival, 5, 7, 8, 9
Great Britain, 7, 31
Greece, Greek, 7, 35, 37, 47, 48, 49, 54, 57, 60, 65
Green Men, 3, 5, 6, 7, 8, 20, 21, 23, 24, 25, 26, 29, 30, 31, 32, 68
griffin, 46, 49, 50, 51, 66
grotesque, 6, 7, 8, 9, 10, 12, 13, 14, 15, 16, 17, 18, 20, 23, 45, 65, 67, 68, 71
guardian, 47, 48, 49, 57, 64, 65, 67

H

horns, 31, 53, 54, 56
Hotel Regis, 54, 55
Howe Apartments, 29

J

Jack-in-the-Green, 22
Jesus, 22, 25, 55, 56

K

Kathleen Basford, 19

L

La Primavera, 84
lions, 48, 50

M

Masonic Temple, 32, 33, 56, 57
Medieval, 7, 12, 13, 21, 24, 26, 35, 43, 49, 65, 66
mermaids, 34, 36, 37, 38, 40, 41, 42, 43, 44
Mesopotamia, 34
Middle Ages, 11, 12, 15-17, 20, 22, 23, 65
Mission San Luis Obispo, 28, 29
Miwok, 39, 63, 64
monsters, 8, 65
Mother Goddess, 47, 58, 61, 64
myth, 5, 65
mythology, 4, 7, 26, 34, 36, 39, 40, 46, 47, 48, 56, 58, 65, 67

N

National Cathedral, 15
National Gold Bank, 47
Native American, 37, 42, 57, 58, 62, 63
Nature, 5, 7, 19, 25, 26, 27, 28, 34, 44, 49
Neo-platonism, 26, 27
New York, 11
Newton Booth, 20, 44, 45
Nigeria, 47
Northstar stone, 63
Norway, 34, 39
Notre-Dame, 8, 10, 11
nymphs, 27, 36

O

oak, 23, 24
offerings, 39, 53, 54
Old Town, 20, 44, 45

P

pagan, 4, 5, 9, 10, 11, 12, 13, 14, 18, 19, 20, 22, 23, 24, 25, 26, 27, 46, 53, 54
pan, 54
Pope Gregory, 14

R

rain rocks, 63
ram, 53, 54, 55, 56, 57
Reformation, 25, 28
religion, 4, 5, 25, 46, 61, 63
resurrection, 47, 60
River Goddess, 37
River Mermaids, 37, 39, 41
River People, 37, 41
Romanesque, 8, 14, 35
Rouen, 55

S

Sacramento, 1, 6, 7, 10, 17, 20, 28, 29, 30, 31, 32, 38, 44, 45, 48, 54, 56, 63, 64, 68, 69, 71
Sacramento Cathedral, 30
sacred wells, 40
Satan, 67

sea goddess, 36, 42
shaman, 60, 62
Sioux, 62
St. Bernard, 10, 13, 14
St. John, 40
Sullivan Building, 17
sun-disk, 53, 56
superstition, 37, 42
symbolism, 4, 5, 8, 11, 14, 19, 21, 23, 26, 46, 49, 52
thunder, 54
tree, 22, 24, 27, 60, 61

U

Udmurt, 41
unicorns, 46

V

vines, 25

W

Wales, 18
Water Spirits, 36-39, 41
Westminster Presbyterian Church, 50, 52, 68

www.ingramcontent.com/pod-product-compliance
Lightning Source LLC
Chambersburg PA
CBHW021229280526
45784CB00005B/2028